Braai
IN
Style

This book is dedicated to all the wonderful friends who have shared the glow of a Snyman fire.

BRAAI
IN
STYLE

LANNICE SNYMAN

PHOTOGRAPHS BY VOLKER MIROS

S&S
PUBLISHERS

ACKNOWLEDGEMENTS

Photographing this book has involved many, many hours of work and I wish to thank the team ...
Marble Mill, Diep River, for the granite and marble backdrops
My daughters, Courtenay and **Tamsin**, for helping with shopping, clearing away and washing up,
and not grumbling about eating at midnight (or not at all)
Angela Miros for keeping the peace, keeping tabs and helping with all aspects
of the propping, styling and photography
My husband, Michael, for designing and making the painted backdrops and
for doing all the braaiing in weather both fair and foul
Volker Miros, photographer, co-braaier, gourmet, friend

PO Box 26344, Hout Bay 7872, South Africa
Tel (021) 790-3367. Fax (021) 790-1055
e-mail: lannice@iafrica.com

First Edition published by Struik Publishers (Pty) Ltd 1993

Second Impression published by S&S Publishers 1999

Reprinted 2001

Text, photographs and illustrations © Lannice Snyman 1993

All rights reserved. No part of this publication may be reproduced, stored in a retrieval system or transmitted,
in any form or by any means, electronic, mechanical, recording or otherwise, without the prior written permission
of the copyright owner and publisher.

Editor: Elaine Hurford
Editorial assistant: Glynne Williamson
Designer: Janice Evans
Cover design: Petal Palmer
Illustrator: Samantha van Riet
Photographer: Volker Miros
Preparation and food styling: Lannice Snyman
Braaiing: Michael Snyman

Typesetting by BellSet, Cape Town

Reproduction by Unifoto (Pty) Ltd., Cape Town

Printed and bound by Tien Wah Press (Pte.) Ltd, Singapore

ISBN 0 620 23840 2

CONTENTS

Author's note 7

Cooking over the coals 9

Starters 13

Meat 19

Beef 25

Venison 29

Lamb 31

Pork 35

Veal 39

Chicken 41

Offal 45

Sausage 47

Seafood 49

The spitroast 57

Potjiekos 61

Sauces and dressings 67

Side dishes 71

Bread 87

Dessert 91

Index 95

Herbed Tomato Sauce (page 68), lamb loin chops, Potbrood (page 62), Foil-Baked Onions (page 76), Cheesy Chicken in Bacon (page 41)

AUTHOR'S NOTE

In wide open spaces taste buds tingle more intensely and hunger pangs are greater in anticipation of The Braai. For many millions of back-yard braaiers the job is decidedly a part-time (if passionate) occupation, often quite commendably accomplished even by those with little or no experience in the art of cooking.

New Braai in Style is for everyone who, like me, loves nothing better than the magic of the fireside, the aromatic sizzle of a chop, and a couple of hours of warm conviviality.

The fabric of this book has been woven from the threads of countless recipes and snippets of information gleaned over many years of braaiing – that most congenial of meal-sharing occasions.

Friends and family have gathered, the flames have died down and glowing coals are ready for action. Experience and gut feeling take over as the time arrives for the skills of the braaier to be put to the test.

My own fireside experiences – mostly happy, a few disastrous, all enlightening – form a broad base of expertise from which I've built a mine of information on all aspects of the art of cooking over the coals.

Though widely varied and suited to braais from casual to ultra-formal, all the recipes have one thing in common – an essence of style to make your braai an occasion to be remembered with pleasure.

Enjoy!

Lannice Snyman

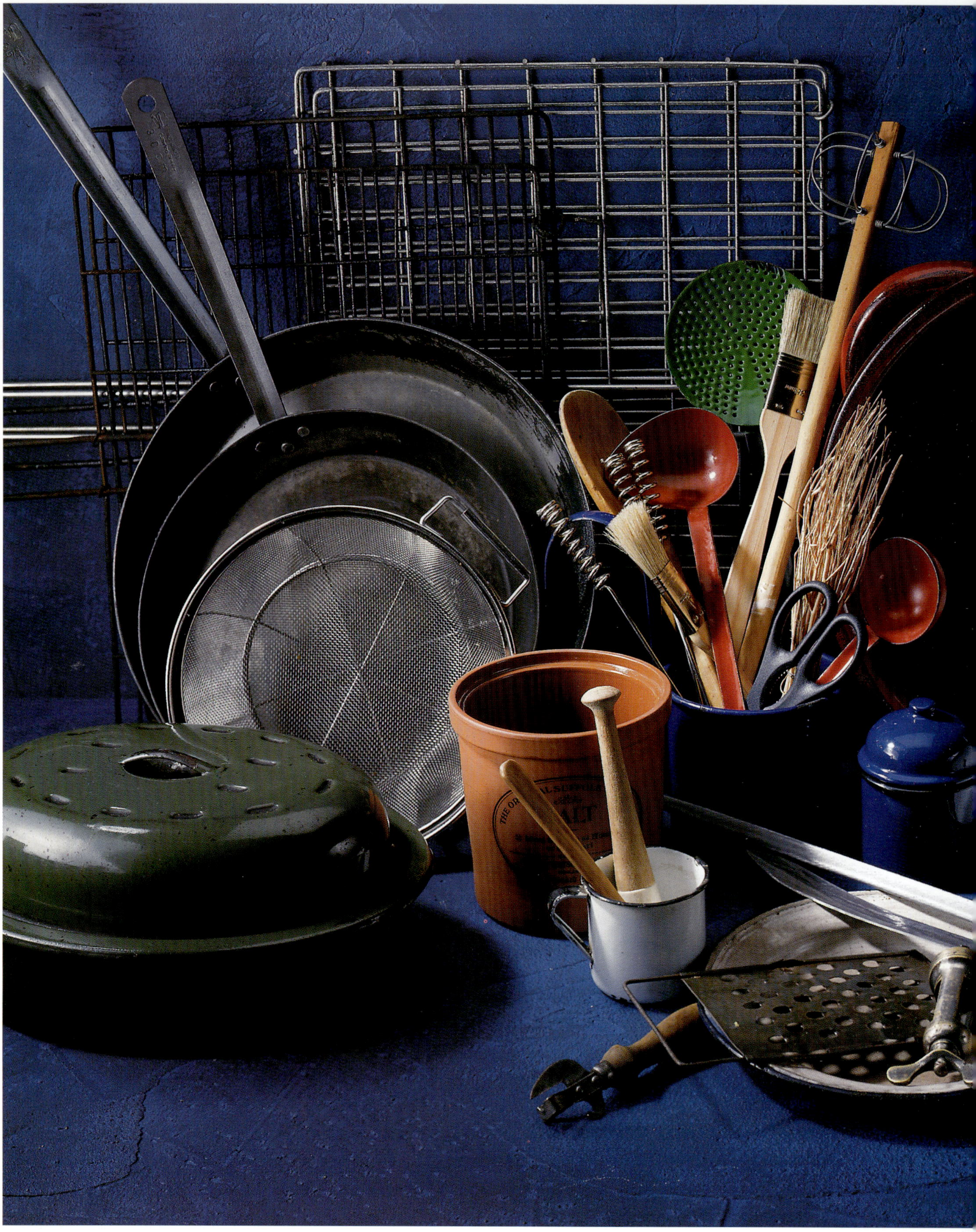

CHAPTER 1

COOKING OVER THE COALS

For those of you who imagine that The Perfect Chop (and by that I mean the whole braai bit – fish, flesh, fowl and accompaniments) earned its capital letters all on its own, read on! A little friendly advice and lots of practice, and you're well on your way to becoming the world's best braaier.

THE FIRE
A successful braai begins with the siting of the fire and ends with flavourful platters of sustenance. In between are a host of matters for consideration – choice of fuel, heat of coals, positioning of grid, supplementary fires to augment the coals and the correct timing of everything to be cooked.

Taking into account the vagaries of man and weather, this is by no means an easy task, and small wonder that a sense of humour (and a little liquid refreshment) plays so vital a part in keeping matters progressing smoothly!

In the open veld or on a deserted beach, ferreting out a place to braai is easy. Siting a home-braai (permanent or mobile) may be a bit more problematical. Prevailing winds, available space, garden layout and proximity to the kitchen (if you don't have a staff of six) must all be taken into account. In the final analysis, though, nothing, it seems, stands in the way of any self-respecting South African making a fire over which to cook.

A selection of utensils for a braai

THE FIRE-BOX
You have two choices: a built-in braai or a portable fire-box – they come in an assortment of sizes, materials and prices. Many families are the proud possessors of both, a permanent arrangement built into a convenient spot plus a mobile contraption for use in inclement weather or when the braai is moved to some far-flung corner of the country.

Among the portable fire-boxes available there's the handy *Hibachi* which originated in Japan and is now popular world wide. *Picnic braais* come in various sizes, the smallest of which fold into boot-sized parcels.

In addition to the conventional fire-boxes, indoor and outdoor *charcoal grills* – gas or electrically operated – are fast gaining popularity as a means of cooking a quick steak.

There are, of course, some folk who happily build their fire in a rusty and rickety wheelbarrow, a sliced-in-twain metal drum, or nestled in an assemblage of stones and bricks. These makeshift arrangements have an added cost advantage besides permitting a nifty size and height change. The addition or subtraction of a few bricks or stones will quickly alter the size to accommodate a couple of extra chops, or allow you to raise or lower the grid to adjust the cooking temperature.

COOKING UNDER A HOOD
Place a dome over what's cooking and the cooking time shortens quite considerably – a factor which is especially useful when preparing a large piece of meat like a leg of lamb or a whole fillet of beef – or even a whole fish. Trap the heat and the food cooks from all sides rather than just from below, leaving the upper surfaces out in the cold.

Zooty imports come in various colours and sizes with an amazing array of attachments. Wheels make them manoeuvrable, even in mid-sizzle if need be. The lids are designed to protect food from the elements while converting the system into an oven, where radiant heat and circulating smoky-hot air turns a braai into a roast in no time.

Briquettes are the ideal fuel, but please remember to let them burn down sufficiently before you cook; there should be a film of grey ash over the surface. Always sear and brown meat with the hood off, then close up, open the draught dampers, and sit back and relax, rising only occasionally to turn the food and check that what you're cooking hasn't been incinerated (a likely event if you haven't allowed the coals to burn low enough beforehand).

Home-made contraptions make good alternatives to the more costly hooded braais. Make a foil dome over a wire framework or simply invert a heat-proof bowl over the meat.

FOIL COOKING OVER THE COALS

Cooking in foil bears no resemblance whatever to braaiing; it's really a steaming or baking process. Nevertheless this contemporary variation of a classic technique — when mealie leaves, banana leaves and seaweed strips were brought into play — has a definite role to play in cooking over the coals. Use it to enhance conventional braaied goodies to widen your repertoire of outdoor recipes. Unlike natural substances, foil is stronger and seals completely. And your parcels can be prepared in advance and refrigerated overnight if necessary.

To allow for even cooking, cut everything the same size and make quite sure there is a good seal. A quick spray of oil will prevent the contents from sticking, and remember to keep the shiny side in to reflect heat rays towards rather than away from the food. Choose heavy foil which more easily withstands the heat.

Don't expect foil-cooked food to have the character of food braaied over open coals. Remember, too, that it's a quick-cooking method, so flavours will remain separate rather than mingle.

If a potato is the only thing you've ever cooked in foil, think again; there are a host of recipes in this book to provide delicious foil-braaied fare.

THE GRID

Flat or hinged? Both serve their purpose equally well. A hinged grid is a boon when braaiing a quantity of the same type of meat of uniform thickness. It allows the food to be turned with a minimum of fuss, gripping everything securely and cutting down on the type of mishap which leaves tasty tit-bits cremating away in the coals. A hinged grid is the answer when braaiing fish, a creature which tends to fall apart more easily than other types of flesh.

On a flat grid each piece of meat may be individually attended to — prodded, turned, basted, tested for done-ness and removed as required. It also allows the portions to be moved from areas of intense heat to cooler parts of the grid if a gentler heat is required.

FUEL FOR COALS

Wood, charcoal, briquettes, dried corn cobs, vine stumps; all — equally happily — end their days as heaps of glowing coals. While not wishing to enter into any altercation with the purists (everyone insists *their* choice of fuel is the best), there's no denying that both the quality and quantity of the coals are vital to the success of any braai.

Whatever your choice, don't skimp on the fuel for your fire. Many's the glow that has petered out and died stone dead before the cooking's done, resulting in a red-faced host, ravenous guests and a harassed hostess streaking indoors to preheat the grill and commence divorce proceedings.

Garner masses of fuel, light the fire in good time and — when handling large quantities of meat or when you have a variety of goodies to cook — do yourself a favour and have a second fire in the process of burning down when the main fire's ready. This way there'll be a supplementary supply of coals just in case they're needed ...

BUILDING A FIRE

Every fire-maker has his own special technique, but the basic idea is to commence operations with crumpled newspaper straddled with thin, dry kindling wood. Once this is alight, add thicker pieces of dry wood, charcoal or briquettes, building up the fire until there's a generous amount of fuel for coals and some left over to cluster around convivially afterwards.

As anyone with the vaguest sense of smell will concede, commercial firelighters should be used with caution. For the same reason it's plain common sense never, ever to use petrol or paraffin to boost the flames. And don't use wood that has been artificially treated with anything noxious or nasty-smelling.

A wind-shield round the blustery side of the fire will prevent it from burning down (and out) too quickly. An added advantage if the weather's chilly, is that the meat cooks more quickly. Some braais have built-in shields, but a portable length of colourful canvas with broomsticks thumped into the ground at intervals certainly won't go amiss.

HEAT OF THE COALS

This is a magic factor governing success or failure in the cooking stakes. They must be hot enough to seal the meat, locking in the juices and flavour, yet not so hot as to burn the outer layer before the inside has reached the ready-point. Then, too, different meat requires different degrees of heat, further testing the skills of the braaier.

Briquettes and charcoal must have reached a stage where they are covered with a fine layer of grey ash (after 30-45 minutes), and a wood fire should have passed the flame stage to a heap of glowing coals. Start braaiing too soon and you'll burn your meat before you have time to down a beer. Wait even longer if the meat requires more gentle heat.

It's common sense to have on hand some form of burn lotion just in case a digit or two gets scorched. Alternatively plunge the part in icy cold water, or plaster it with butter or margarine.

MANAGING A BRAAI

If the whole affair is badly managed one is so often rewarded with either a bloody sacrifice or a burnt offering.

Advance preparation is essential for a braai when one would rather be enjoying the company than fussing around in the kitchen. Decide beforehand just how simple or elaborate your 'do' is to be and get all the chores done in advance. Consider the visual appeal. Plan platters and garnishes in advance, raid the garden for suitable greenery, leaving the hackneyed sprigs of parsley for lesser occasions, and scoff-serving can be accomplished prettily and effortlessly.

It's braaiing time. Experience takes over from science as decisions are made which affect a perfect end-product. How far from the coals to cook; the length of the cooking time; basting and turning the meat; the varying cooking times for each item, aiming always to have everything ready simultaneously.

The sound of the sizzle is a pretty good indication of the cooking temperature, and the resistance of the meat to a well-aimed prod indicates the degree of done-ness. A lot of practice and a little bravado makes perfect. Trial and error are good tutors, so the more often you braai the better you'll get.

SERVING THE FEAST

Braaied foods don't take kindly to being kept waiting between the cooking and the eating stages, so it's very important to regulate the timing of everything to be served – the braaied goodies and the side dishes waiting in the wings. Have everything ready for action when the last morsel leaves the grid.

When the cooking's done and the feasting begins, pile wood on the fire. Nothing can compare with the crackling blaze and the ambience it creates, drawing everyone into the circle of its friendly glow. An electric light bulb simply cannot compare for magic.

For the last word in pampering, wrap small dampened towels in foil. Warm them round the edge of the fire and pass them around to fix sticky fingers.

The flames die down to a heap of glowing coals, ready for action

COOKING OVER THE COALS

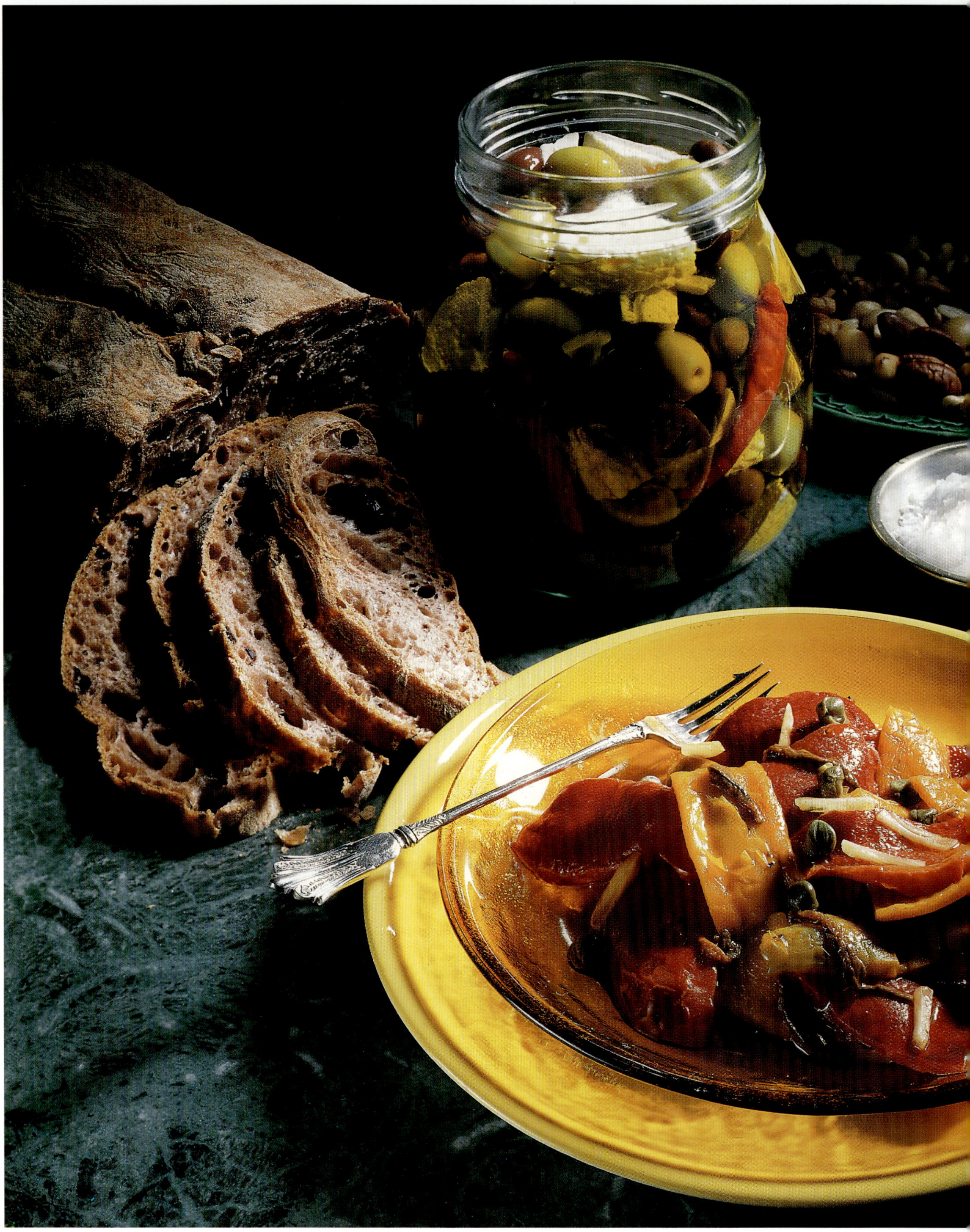

CHAPTER 2

STARTERS

Fire-watching may be loads of fun, so is a casual gathering of family and friends and a smattering of stimulating conversation. But all this will not keep the hunger pangs at bay.

This selection of starters has been designed to be served with a minimum of fuss, involving the barest essentials in the way of crockery and cutlery. Many of the recipes are easily transportable and may be mixed and matched to suit the size of the gathering. They have the added advantage of advance preparation, leaving you free for the more pleasurable pursuits of socialising and relaxing.

MARINATED OLIVES AND FETA

Make a large batch to keep on hand in the fridge; they'll be perfect for several weeks. Bring to room temperature and offer as snacks or scatter them over a salad. Always remember to use good quality olive oil.

500 g green olives
500 g black olives
400 g feta cheese, cut into blocks
4 cloves garlic, skinned and halved
15 ml whole coriander, lightly crushed
2 fresh red or green chillies, halved and seeded
few sprig-tips of fresh rosemary
olive oil

Marinated Olives and Feta,
Roasted Mixed Nuts (page 13),
Italian Peppers with Anchovies (page 16)

Drain olives and place in a bowl with the feta cheese, garlic, coriander, chillies and rosemary. Toss gently to mix. Repack the jars – or fill one large jar – and fill to the brim with olive oil. Seal and refrigerate until required.
Makes 1,5 kg

ROASTED MIXED NUTS

These aromatic nibbles may be roasted over the coals or in the oven and served as they cool down. Mix and match according to your fancy; choose from peanuts, cashews, brazils, almonds, walnuts, hazelnuts, pinenuts and macadamias.

500 g mixed nuts, shelled
salt

Preheat oven to 180 °C. Scatter the nuts in a roasting pan, add a sprinkling of salt and roast for about 20 minutes, tossing them about every 5 minutes or so until they are evenly brown. Watch carefully – they burn quick as lick.

When roasting on the fire, make sure your coals are coolish and roast the salted nuts in a large, heavy frying pan, turning them constantly so they brown evenly without the risk of burning.

If, by some miracle, there are some left over, store in a screw-topped jar in the fridge to enjoy at a later date.
Serves 6-10

Szechwan Cucumbers, Fresh Asparagus with Citrus Mayonnaise (page 15)

14 STARTERS

SZECHWAN CUCUMBERS

Hauntingly flavoured fingerlets of cucumber marinated in a hot and pungent oriental mix. They keep perfectly for up to 2 weeks in the fridge. Szechwan peppercorns are available from speciality Chinese merchants. Substitute white or black peppercorns if you can't find the real thing.

1 large English cucumber
salt

SZECHWAN DRESSING
10 ml sesame oil
5 ml finely chopped green ginger
   or 2 ml ground ginger
2 fresh green or red chillies, seeded
   and finely shredded
5 ml Szechwan peppercorns
30 ml wine vinegar
15 ml brown sugar

Slice cucumber lengthwise into 8 strips. Remove pips and slice strips into 5 cm pieces. Place in a bowl, sprinkle with salt and set aside for about 30 minutes. The salt will draw out the excess moisture.

Tip cucumber into a colander, rinse with cold water, drain and pat dry. Transfer to a serving bowl.

Heat sesame oil in a frying pan and stir-fry ginger, chilli and peppercorns for about 20 seconds. Add vinegar and sugar and stir until sugar dissolves. Pour the hot dressing over the cucumber and toss to mix. Cover and refrigerate for at least 6 hours (overnight is even better), before serving.
Serves 8-10

FRESH ASPARAGUS WITH CITRUS MAYONNAISE

Fresh asparagus is one of the best tastes of summer, and it makes a delicious, easy-to-eat starter either as is with a scattering of milled pepper and a squeeze of lemon, or with the perfect partner of this unusual mayonnaise.

2 punnets asparagus

CITRUS MAYONNAISE
3 egg yolks
1 ml salt
1 ml dry English mustard
30 ml lemon juice
45 ml orange juice
grated rind of 1 orange
375 ml sunflower oil

Wash asparagus and cut off a thin slice from the cut end. Slim green spears need no trimming but the skin of larger spears tends to be a little coarse, so they should be peeled. Do this with a vegetable peeler or a very sharp knife, working from the base towards the bud.

Ultra-slim spears may be steamed over boiling water; plumper specimens should be boiled. If you have a correctly proportioned pot stand them upright in the water, the buds standing clear to steam. Alternatively lie them flat in a covered saucepan and simmer until tender – they should droop just a little when lifted. Drain asparagus and arrange on a serving plate.

MAYONNAISE Place yolks, salt and mustard into the bowl of a food processor or mixer and whisk until thick and pale. With the machine running, slowly add lemon juice, orange juice and rind, then add the oil very slowly in a thin, thin stream. Scoop it into a bowl and serve as a dunking sauce.
Serves 6-8

MAKE AHEAD
Asparagus is ideally served freshly cooked and slightly warm or at room temperature. The mayonnaise may be stored for up to 5 days in the fridge but make sure it's well sealed.

ARTICHOKES WITH BALSAMIC VINAIGRETTE

An easy, elegant pre-braai snack, which may be prepared up to a day ahead and refrigerated. Remember, though, that the flavour is at its peak at room temperature so take the artichokes out of the fridge in good time.

12 small artichokes
125 ml dry white wine
60 ml olive oil
3-4 garlic cloves, peeled and chopped
1 bay leaf
2 sprigs thyme
3 sprigs parsley
6 peppercorns
1 ml salt

BALSAMIC VINAIGRETTE
125 ml olive oil
30 ml wine vinegar
30 ml balsamic vinegar
1 ml salt
1 ml sugar
milled black pepper

Trim artichoke bases, remove toughest outer leaves and, if you feel that their appearance could handle a little improving, cut off the top third of the leaves. Clean by running cold water into them, then set aside for an hour or so in a bowl of salted cold water. This will get rid of any nasties that could be lurking about.

Place artichokes upright in a deep saucepan with cold water to cover and wine, olive oil, garlic, herbs, peppercorns and salt. Cover and simmer gently until tender. This could take anything from 15-45 minutes depending on their size. They are ready if tender when pierced with a thin skewer, or as soon as the outer leaves feel as if they're ready to pull free.

Allow artichokes to cool in the cooking liquid, then drain and arrange on a serving plate. Mix vinaigrette ingredients together, pour into the leaves and set the dish aside to marinate for a couple of hours. Garnish with nasturtium flowers and leaves.
Serves 6

STARTERS 15

ITALIAN PEPPERS WITH ANCHOVIES

A colourful, brilliantly flavoured Mediterranean treat, which keeps for up to a week in the fridge.

3 large red peppers
3 large yellow peppers
45 ml olive oil
4-5 cloves garlic, very finely slivered
12 anchovy fillets
45 ml capers
sea salt and milled black pepper

Char the skins of the peppers under the oven griller or over a gas flame. Enclose in a plastic bag to 'sweat', then remove the skin. Slice peppers into strips, discard seeds and ribs and place in a bowl. Add remaining ingredients, toss well and pile into a bowl.
Serves 6

VARIATION
A selection of blanched vegetables may be added to the peppers – try cauliflower or broccoli florets, button mushrooms, slim green beans, chunks of leek – even new potatoes cooked in their jackets.

ITALIAN ANTIPASTO

A brilliant array of tastebud-zapping finger-food has loads of visual and flavour impact. With it, offer well-chilled red nouveau-style wine. My favourite combination of goodies includes many of the recipes in this selection of starters, together with an array of deli lines like …

sliced meats such as mortadella, pastrami and ham
piles of glistening black olives
infant tomatoes
fresh, ripe radishes
blanched baby green beans glossed with vinaigrette
selection of sliced and cubed cheese

Arrange it all beautifully on a large tray or platter and offer with slices of hot, crusty bread.

HERBED CHICKEN LIVER PÂTÉ

There was a time when pâté was the most popular starter in town. While it may have lost some of its fashion-appeal, pâté is still an ideal pre-braai offering to serve with salty biscuits, triangles of toast or home-made bread.

250 g chicken livers
1 small onion, chopped
200 g butter
15 ml chopped fresh herbs (thyme, origanum, marjoram) or 2 ml dried mixed herbs
salt and milled black pepper
30 ml brandy
30 ml dry sherry
30 ml chopped parsley
60 ml cream

Wash chicken livers, cut off and discard any nasty bits and pieces and pat dry.
Sauté onion in a little of the butter until soft but not browned. Stir in chopped herbs (not the parsley), salt and plenty of pepper, then add livers. Fry, stirring and turning, until just done.
Purée the mixture in a blender or food processor with remaining butter, brandy, sherry, parsley and cream. Check seasoning then pour into a serving bowl, cover and chill.
Makes 500 ml

VARIATION
Instead of herbs use 15 ml lightly crushed green peppercorns.

MAKE AHEAD
The pâté may be prepared up to 3 days ahead, and will last even longer if covered with clarified butter. Melt it, pour over a thin layer and chill to set.

CLARIFIED BUTTER
The best pâté topper and ideal for frying, as it doesn't burn.
Bring 500 g butter to a gentle boil in a deep saucepan. Cook uncovered over low heat for about 10 minutes. During this time the water will evaporate, sediment will rise to the surface, salt will settle and the clarified butter will remain in the middle.
Allow to cool, then gently scrape off the sediment and lift the clarified butter from the salt. Keep refrigerated.

TOMATO AND MOZZARELLA WITH BASIL VINAIGRETTE

Simplicity is the key here but the quality of the ingredients is of prime importance. If basil is unavailable, substitute another fresh herb like tarragon, thyme or origanum. On no account use dried herbs; you'll ruin the dish.

6 firm, ripe tomatoes, sliced
300 g mozzarella cheese, thinly sliced
small bunch chives, finely sliced (optional)
small basil sprigs or leaves

BASIL VINAIGRETTE
60 ml olive oil
30 ml wine vinegar
5 ml soy sauce
squeeze of lemon juice
6-8 fresh basil leaves, finely chopped
salt and milled black pepper

Arrange sliced tomato and mozzarella in overlapping circles on a flattish platter and top with chives. Mix vinaigrette ingredients together and drizzle over the top. Garnish with basil.
Serves 6-8

MAKE AHEAD
This salad may be sealed with clingfilm and refrigerated for an hour or two. If preparing it even further ahead, add the dressing just before serving.

STARTERS

HOT TOMATO TOASTS

Toast the bruschetta over the coals and have the topping simmering on the sidelines. If basil isn't in season, use fresh tarragon or marjoram. Make sure, too, that your tomatoes are ripe and bursting with flavour. If not add a dash of tomato paste.

8-10 slices Bruschetta (page 88)

TOPPING
500 g very ripe cocktail tomatoes, halved
2-3 cloves garlic, crushed
8 large basil leaves, very finely sliced
pinch of sugar
salt and milled black pepper

The topping may be prepared several days in advance and reheated when necessary. Combine the ingredients in a small saucepan, seasoning to taste with salt, pepper and a touch of sugar. Simmer uncovered until mushy and thickened. Prepare bruschetta and serve directly from the grid, spooning the topping on while the toast is still hot.

Serves 6-8

Hot Tomato Toasts

STARTERS 17

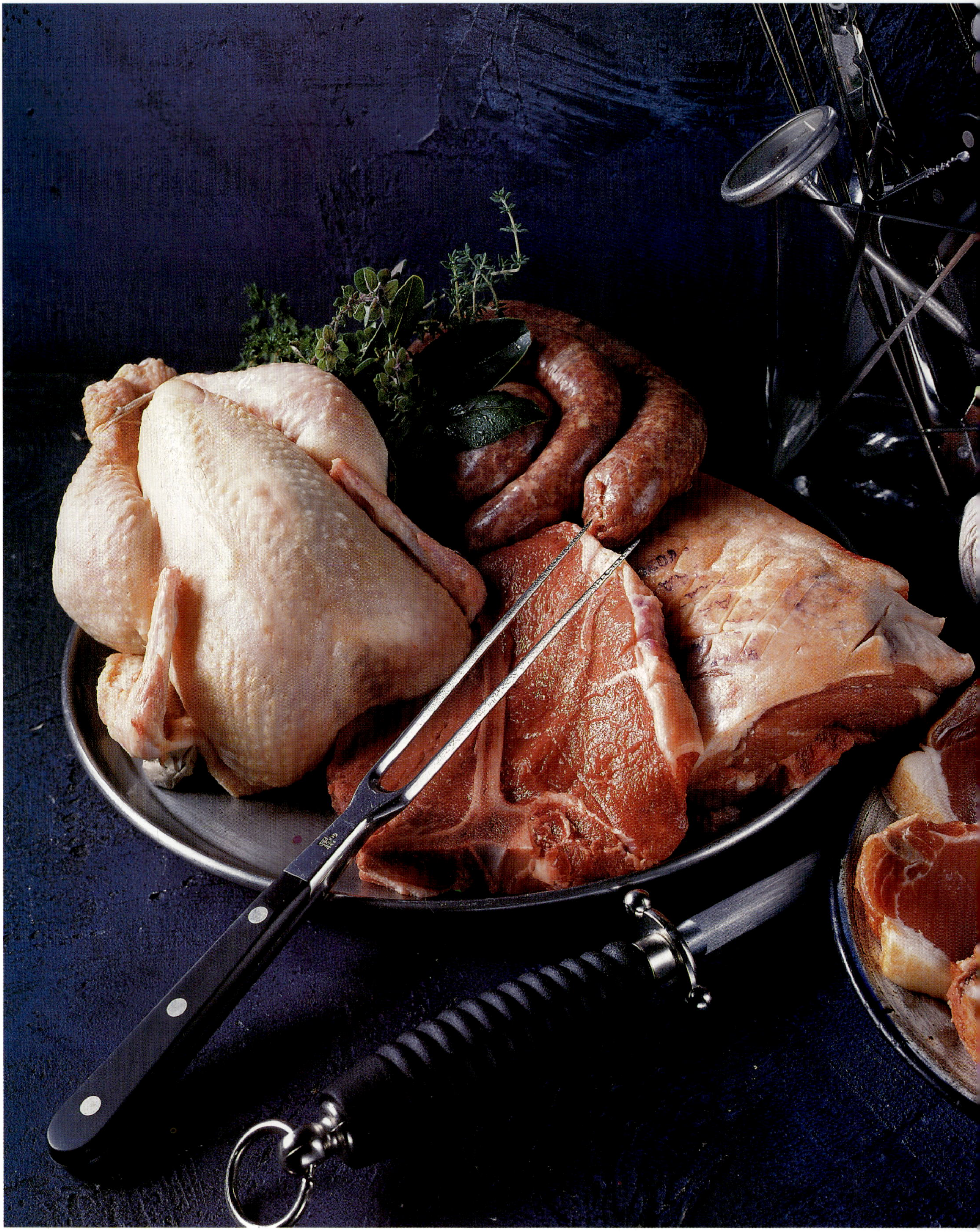

CHAPTER 3

MEAT

Meat – almost always the focal point of the feast – requires infinite care to be taken in its choice, maturing and flavouring, and a great deal of loving care in its cooking and presentation.

CHOICE
Now that pristine and tempting displays of meat are to be found in every food store, the friendly family butcher has all but disappeared from the scene. However there are still many of the cleaver-wielding fraternity who will happily take time off to give advice on all aspects of the subject.

Braaiing is a dry method of cooking so don't expect the miracle of meat becoming more tender as it cooks. If anything it will toughen, especially if overcooked. Only long, slow, moist methods of cooking can claim to tenderise meat. It is vital, therefore, that one chooses suitable cuts for braaiing and handles them properly.

RIPENING (MATURING)
Beef and lamb should be ripened before braaiing. This may have been done by your butcher before he carved up the carcass, but he may not have done so. Find out; it is vital to the tenderness of the meat. There are two ways of doing it. Traditionally a whole or half carcass is hung in a cool room. Alternatively smaller portions of meat (like a whole rump) may be laid on the rack of the fridge. Forget about trying to ripen chops or steak – they'll simply shrivel up. Store the meat at a temperature of 0-4 °C (the temperature of a household fridge); beef for 7-14 days, lamb for 2-7 days.

Plump chicken, boerewors, loin of lamb, T-bone steak, gammon chops

Wipe meat with a vinegar-soaked cloth and make certain that it's free of any bone dust. This will cause the meat to go off. Never rinse meat under running water or allow it to languish in a water-filled sink. You'll wash away nutrients and a certain amount of blood, which will cause the meat to toughen.

Vacuum-packing is a newer concept in ripening meat in the fridge, ensuring that it is hermetically sealed in thick plastic impervious to oxygen and humidity. It ripens beautifully in this atmosphere, with minimum weight-loss.

FREEZING
Careless freezing and thawing can ruin the most superb meat, so here are a few common-sense comments.
- ☐ Freeze only meat that is matured, cleaned and trimmed of excess fat, sinews and bones.
- ☐ Cut into serving portions.
- ☐ Pack well in durable freezer-wrap and label clearly.
- ☐ Freeze as quickly as possible or you'll run the risk of the formation of ice-crystals which damage the meat fibres. Professional blast-freezing solves this problem. Having a quick-freeze compartment in your domestic freezer helps, as does keeping parcels as flat as possible. And, of course, never overcrowd the freezer.
- ☐ To prevent loss of moisture, defrost slowly overnight in the fridge or at room temperature. If you simply must speed up the defrosting process, lie the plastic-wrapped portions in cold water, or use the defrost cycle of your microwave oven.
- ☐ Stick to the freezing time-limits; beef, lamb and game for up to one year; pork, veal, minced meat and offal for up to six months; sausage for up to two months.

MEAT OVER THE COALS

Consider its appearance. Trim away sinews, lop off the more unsightly bones, remove excess fat, leaving just sufficient to add flavour. In order to prevent chops and steaks from curling on the grid, score through the fat at intervals of 2-3 cm.

Always bring meat to room temperature before braaiing, then there'll be no need to rely on guesswork as far as cooking time is concerned.

Unless you actually like dried-out meat, ban all forks from the braai. To retain the juices avoid puncturing meat. Turn with tongs.

Oil your grid and the meat before braaiing to prevent the two sticking together. Quickly sear meat on both sides to seal in the juices. While braaiing turn frequently to ensure even browning and even cooking.

Time the cooking procedure, aiming to have everything ready at once. Take cognisance of the various cooking times and add the various types of meat to the grid timeously.

Learn to cook to perfection. Listen to the sizzle — it's a sure indication of both the heat and the cooking speed. Learn, furthermore, by the feel of the meat when prodded, when it's done to the desired degree.

Cooking by intuition is finally the test of the expert. It is impossible to give timing rules, as so much affects the issue: the thickness and temperature of the meat before it's placed on the grid, the heat of the fire and the temperature of the air and errant breezes. In the end it's up to you!

FLAVOURING

Between the extremes of a miser's touch of salt and marinating meat beyond human understanding are many exciting flavouring possibilities.

Surface flavouring. A light flavouring of the outer surface of the meat with herbs and spices, a cut clove of garlic or a squeeze of lemon juice is delicious, as is a brushing of Worcestershire, soy or a basting sauce. These seasonings won't have time to penetrate too far, but the appearance and flavour will be greatly enhanced.

Meat is not normally spiced too far ahead of time. Salt, pepper, herbs and spices draw out the natural juices.

Marinating and basting places meat in a different league. Some purists shun the practice, being of the opinion that if the cut, quality and maturity is good, additional flavouring is unnecessary, overpowering rather than enhancing the flavour. They are correct up to a point, but there are those tougher cuts which benefit greatly from the marinating process. Besides, one can conjure up many enjoyable flavour variations.

The reasons for marinating are:
☐ Flavour penetration, which is governed by the flavouring agents and the duration of the marinating time.
☐ Tenderising of the meat by including wine, vinegar or beer.
☐ Preservation of the meat, which was essential in days before the advent of the fridge and cooler-box. Nowadays this factor assumes importance mainly on camping trips once the cooler-box has lost its cool.

Some marinades burn easily over the coals, a risk that could be lessened if the meat is patted dry before braaiing. One can also increase the distance between the coals and the meat, and it also helps to turn the meat frequently.

The duration of the marinating time depends on the type of meat, the size of the cut and the flavour penetration desired. Large joints may be marinated for anything from several hours to several days. Sosaties, kebabs and tougher cuts may be steeped in the flavouring for between one and five days.

Chicken responds well to being marinated for several hours or a couple of days. Flavour penetration is aided and braaiing time is reduced by par-cooking chicken in the marinade. Venison and ribs may be marinated for a day or two, and ribs also benefit by par-cooking.

Chops and steak, on the other hand, are best when their natural flavour is preserved, though a quick lick with a basting sauce never goes amiss.

Fish is flavoursome, tender and (mostly) moist, so marinate only to add flavour. Use gentle flavours and a short marinating time — an hour or two at most.

SEASONING

Here's where prudence and expertise go hand in hand. To lift dishes from the mundane into the memorable league, use with discretion the vast array of seasoning agents available.

Wherever possible, choose fresh herbs in preference to dried ones; in each case the quantities for both have been given. And sometimes using the dried commodity is just not on.

Keep an eye on your dried herbs for signs of ageing. Sniff before use to make sure they're fresh and aromatic. Lengthen their shelf-life by storing dried herbs tightly sealed in a cool, dark place.

With salt and pepper you're in a danger zone; how much to add is a very personal matter and fanatics may add more if they wish. The three types of peppercorns most often used are black, white and green. Freshly milled black pepper is the happiest choice. By comparison ready-ground pepper pales into insignificance. White peppercorns (the inner core of the corns and a trifle less flavoursome than their darker counterparts) may be used when the appearance of the dish may be spoilt by black flecks.

Soft green ones are harvested before the berries are ripe and have a distinctive and pungent bite.

Mustard presents problems of its own as the choice is bewildering. Dijon has been synonymous with fine mustard for centuries and mustards of the type made in this ancient French city are acknowledged as the finest for all purposes. Always use the tongue-shrivelling English mustard with discretion — just a smidgen is usually plenty.

Pork spareribs marinating in Herbs and Honey mixture (page 22)

MEAT

SEVEN SPICE MIX

This blend of spices gives a fairly pungent surface-seasoning, so use sparingly and brush off the excess before braaiing. Add a little salt afterwards.

2 dried bay leaves, finely crumbled
30 ml milled black pepper
10 ml grated nutmeg
10 ml ground paprika
10 ml ground cinnamon
10 ml dried origanum
5 ml ground cloves

Combine the ingredients in a screw-topped jar, shake to mix and store in a cool dark spot. The mixture remains fresh for up to 4 weeks. Store for up to 6 months in the freezer.
Makes about 80 ml

ROASTED BRAAI SPICE

A seductive spice blend to rub into meat. Remember to add a light sprinkling of salt after the meat has been browned or just before serving it.

15 ml cumin seeds
10 ml whole coriander seeds
10 ml whole cardamom seeds
10 ml black peppercorns
10 ml dried juniper berries
6 whole cloves
5 ml garlic flakes
5 ml ground turmeric

In a frying pan combine cumin, coriander, cardamom, peppercorns, juniper berries, cloves and garlic flakes. Toast over medium heat for about 3 minutes, tossing them about until lightly browned and aromatic. Stir in turmeric and grind the spices in a pestle and mortar. Strain to discard the husks and store in a screw-topped jar.
  Use within 4 weeks, or freeze for up to 6 months. The flavours tend to diminish as time goes by after the spices have been ground.
Makes about 50 ml

GARLIC BUTTER

Butter, garlic and lemon juice – perfect partners for basting anything from vegetables to seafood and chicken. Herbs add an extra special touch. Use any of your favourites, fresh from the garden.

3-4 cloves garlic, crushed
200 g butter
finely grated rind and juice of 1 lemon
salt and milled black pepper
30 ml chopped parsley

Sizzle garlic in hot butter for a minute or so, then mix in lemon rind and juice and seasoning to taste. Remove from the heat and stir in chopped parsley.
Makes 250 ml

VARIATION
To add colour and a dash of spice to the recipe, mix in about 30 ml soy or Worcestershire sauce.

MAKE AHEAD
Always have Garlic Butter on hand in the fridge (it is fine for up to a week) or in the freezer, where it may be stored quite happily for several months.

HERBS AND HONEY

A delicate, uncooked mix which subtly influences lamb, chicken, pork or veal.

340 ml bottle beer
125 ml apple juice
125 ml sunflower oil
80 ml honey
60 ml tarragon or wine vinegar
30 ml Dijon mustard
1 small onion, very finely chopped
sprigs of tarragon
15 ml chopped parsley

Combine ingredients and heat just long enough to melt the honey – do this in a small saucepan or in a bowl in the microwave oven. For the delicate flavours to penetrate, marinate meat for several hours and chicken for at least 12 hours.
Makes about 700 ml

PEACHY MARINADE AND BASTING SAUCE

A marinade and basting sauce that goes well with meat that enjoys a sweetish tang: chicken, pork, veal – even fillet steak or lamb chops.

1 small onion, finely chopped
2 cloves garlic, crushed
60 ml olive oil
250 ml semi-sweet white wine
125 ml peach nectar
60 ml medium sherry
30 ml chutney
30 ml vinegar
30 ml mild mustard
5 ml salt

In a small saucepan soften onion and garlic in olive oil. Mix in remaining ingredients, cover and simmer for about 5 minutes. Allow to cool before using as a marinade and baste the meat as it cooks. If there is any left over, reheat it gently, pour it into a bowl and offer as a separate sauce.
Makes about 600 ml

MEDITERRANEAN HERB AND ORANGE BASTE

A citrus flavoured basting sauce especially suited to fish, chicken, pork or veal.

80 ml olive or sunflower oil
grated rind of 1 orange
juice of 3 oranges
grated rind and juice of 1 lemon
6-8 orange or lemon leaves, bruised
2 cloves garlic, chopped
15 ml snipped chives
15 ml chopped parsley
few sprigs fresh origanum
  or 5 ml dried origanum
salt and milled black pepper

Combine all ingredients and use to baste meat before and during cooking.
Makes about 200 ml

SIZZLING MARINADE AND BASTING SAUCE

A flavoursome brew for beef, lamb and chicken – or for anything that requires a major flavour boost.

1 onion, thinly sliced
2 cloves garlic, crushed
60 ml sunflower oil
125 ml wine vinegar
125 ml dry red wine
125 ml tomato sauce
125 ml orange juice
45 ml honey or brown sugar
45 ml Worcestershire sauce
5 ml paprika
10 drops Tabasco
1 small lemon, thinly sliced
salt and milled black pepper

Soften onion and garlic in oil, mix in remaining ingredients, cover and simmer for about 15 minutes. Remove lemon slices and cool the marinade before use.
Makes about 650 ml

MANDARIN MARINADE

Oriental accents predominate in a blend of flavours which are truly tantalising for beef, a treat for ribs and guaranteed to make a chicken chuckle.

60 ml sunflower oil
1 onion, finely chopped
2 cloves garlic, crushed
10 ml finely chopped green ginger
    or 5 ml ground ginger
125 ml orange juice
80 ml wine vinegar
45 ml soy sauce
45 ml tomato sauce
30 ml dry sherry
30 ml brown sugar

Heat oil and sauté onion, garlic and ginger until tender and just starting to brown. Add remaining ingredients, cover and simmer for 5 minutes. Cool.
Makes about 375 ml

Mediterranean Herb and Orange Baste (page 22)

MEAT 23

Marinated Beef Fillet (page 25) served with Figs in Bacon (page 74)

24 MEAT

BEEF

Beef can be the very best – or the very worst – braaied meat. It tests not only the skills of the braaier, but also requires more than just a cursory knowledge of selection, maturation and preparation. For fuller details on these important issues, see page 19.

Various cuts are ideal for braaiing: fillet (whole or in steaks), rump steaks, sirloin steaks, T-bone, porterhouse (entrecôte) steaks, club steaks and the cheaper forequarter cuts of rib-eye steaks, prime rib and flat rib, which are best marinated and may be parboiled prior to braaiing.

The ideal thickness for steak and chops is 2-3 cm which allows a crisp outer surface and tender, succulent interior. Thinner slivers tend to dry out over the coals.

Trim meat before braaiing, removing sinews and excess fat. Score the outer band of fat to prevent the meat buckling up over the heat, and anoint with oil to prevent it from sticking to the grid.

Don't season too long ahead – just before cooking or after browning is best. This will prevent the spices drawing out the meat's juices. Marinate or baste as you prefer. See recipes from page 22.

Always braai beef very quickly over coals that are as hot as hell. Do it slowly over dying embers and you're assured of tough steak. And, you'll ruin it by keeping it warm for too long before serving. This is quite a problem if steak is being cooked in the company of other meats which require longer, slower cooking. To solve this problem have a second fire on the go to provide hot coals for the steak.

Never pierce, stab or prick beef while braaiing – again for reasons of moisture loss. Seal quickly by browning on both sides, then turn frequently enough to prevent bubbles of moisture appearing on the upper surface. These juices must be trapped within the meat for the most succulent results. For the same reason serve steak rare or medium-rare, allow it to settle for a few minutes before serving and carve across the grain of the meat into thickish slices.

MARINATED BEEF FILLET

Fillet is the ultimate in braaied meat. It's costly, for sure, but there's no wastage. For the tenderest meat possible, get your butcher to vacuum-pack it for you and refrigerate it at home for a couple of weeks prior to braaiing.

1,5-2 kg whole beef fillet
salt and milled black pepper

MARINADE
60 ml sunflower or olive oil
125 ml orange juice
3 rashers bacon, finely sliced
30 ml Worcestershire sauce
125 ml dry white wine
2 cloves garlic, crushed
15 ml chopped parsley
   or 5 ml dried parsley
10 ml chopped marjoram
   or 1 ml dried marjoram
juice of 1 small lemon
milled black pepper

Trim fillet and place in a non-metal dish. Mix marinade ingredients, pour over meat and leave to stand at room temperature for 3-4 hours (or overnight in the fridge), turning occasionally.

When your coals are ready for action, remove meat from marinade, pat dry with kitchen paper and season with salt and pepper. Brown well over hot coals, then raise the grid away from the heat to cook at a more moderate rate, basting frequently with remaining marinade.

Your steak will be medium-rare in about 40 minutes. Allow a little longer if you prefer well-done meat; for rare beef, remove fillet from the grid sooner. The internal temperature of medium-rare beef is 60 °C. Allow steak to rest for a few minutes before carving.

Serve with a sauce of your choice accompanied by baked potatoes with sour cream and snipped chives.
Serves 6-8

GARLIC T-BONE

Just the thing for lovers of the pungent clove. If the constitution allows, serve Coal-Roasted Garlic (page 78) on the side.

4 T-bone steaks
1 large clove garlic, peeled and halved
salt and milled black pepper

GARLIC BUTTER
125 g soft butter
3-4 cloves garlic, crushed
good squeeze of lemon juice
milled black pepper

Mix ingredients together for garlic butter, form into a roll and wrap in waxed paper. Refrigerate and chill until hard.

Rub surfaces of the steaks with the cut clove of garlic and season with plenty of pepper. Braai over medium-hot coals until done, seasoning with salt after the meat is browned.

Top each steak with a pat of garlic butter before serving.
Serves 4

MEAT 25

STEAKS WITH BLUE CHEESE STUFFING

Use your favourite steak for this recipe – rump, sirloin (entrecôte), rib-eye or fillet. The stuffed steaks may be refrigerated for up to a day.

4 steaks, 3-4 cm thick
salt and milled black pepper

STUFFING
120 g blue cheese, finely crumbled
20 ml mild mustard
squeeze of lemon juice
30 ml chopped parsley
 or 2 ml dried parsley
2 slices bread, crumbled

Cut a lengthwise slit into the steaks to form a pocket. Season the insides with salt and pepper, mix the stuffing ingredients together, fill the pockets and secure with toothpicks.

Braai steaks crisply on both sides over hot coals, then cook over a more gentle heat until done to the desired degree. Season with salt and pepper after browning. Remove toothpicks and serve with lemon wedges for squeezing.
Serves 4

VARIATION
If you're not mad about blue cheese, use grated mozzarella.

RUMP STEAK WITH OLIVE AND ANCHOVY BUTTER

A pretty powerful treatment for flavourful rump. The butter may be refrigerated for a week. It also freezes well.

4 thick rump steaks
salt and milled black pepper
olive oil

OLIVE AND ANCHOVY BUTTER
125 g soft butter
10 black olives, stones removed
6 anchovy fillets

Whiz all ingredients for the olive and anchovy butter in a food processor, seasoning to taste with milled black pepper. Chill until serving time.

Season steaks with pepper and brush with olive oil. Braai over hot coals until well browned and done to your liking. Turn frequently.

Serve steaks directly from the grid, topping each one with a dollop of the flavoured butter.
Serves 4

INDONESIAN SATAY

Spicy satay are the forerunners of our much-loved local sosatie. Beef, lamb or game are best in this recipe, and pork and chicken may be used as well but the character of the spices will ultimately dominate the flavour of the meat.

1 kg lean meat
salt

INDONESIAN MARINADE
60 ml sunflower oil
1 onion, finely chopped
5 ml crushed garlic
2 ml red masala or chilli powder
15 ml peanut butter
10 ml ground turmeric
5 ml brown sugar
45 ml soy sauce
15 ml lemon juice
200 ml water

Slice meat thinly across the grain. (Easiest to do when the meat is semi-frozen as slices should be about 5 mm thick.)
MARINADE In a small saucepan soften onion and garlic in oil. Stir in remaining ingredients, cover and simmer for about 5 minutes. Allow to cool, then pour over the meat, coating it nicely. Cover and marinate for at least 2 hours before threading the meat onto thin bamboo skewers. Retain the marinade and reheat it as it makes a delicious sauce.

Braai satay over hot coals, turning frequently to crisp evenly. Salt lightly before serving with rice and the remaining marinade as a sauce.
Serves 6

HOMESPUN HAMBURGERS

Delicious, economical and versatile. They also will wait patiently in the fridge (interleaved with waxed paper) for 2-3 days, or in the freezer for 6 months.

1 kg minced beef
1 onion, very finely chopped
1 egg, lightly beaten
1 fat clove garlic, crushed
30 ml chopped parsley
 or 10 ml dried parsley
5 ml salt
milled black pepper

Combine all ingredients and form into 8 plump patties. They should be slightly larger than bread rolls as they shrink while cooking. Handle the mixture gently; packing it too tightly makes the burgers tough.

Brush a hinged grid generously with oil and pack in the patties. Sear them quickly on both sides over hot coals, then continue cooking at a more moderate pace until done. About 15 minutes should be sufficient, as burgers are most succulent while still slightly pink inside. Turn occasionally as needs be.

Serve in hot buttered rolls, garnished as desired. See the list given on page 27.
Makes 8

VARIATIONS
ECONO-BURGERS Cheating is permissible to stretch the budget! To the recipe add 250 ml fresh white or brown breadcrumbs and your guests will be none the wiser.

SPICY BURGERS A touch of Worcestershire or soy sauce, chutney or mustard, livens up burgers no end, as does a dash of dried spice. Try curry powder, cumin, allspice or nutmeg.

CHEESE BURGERS Add 250 ml grated Cheddar cheese, 30 ml prepared mustard and 5 ml paprika.

HAWAIIAN BURGERS While your burgers are braaiing toast fresh or tinned pineapple rings on the grid, to pop into the roll with the patty.

HAMBURGER GARNISHES
- ☐ Cool, crisp lettuce leaves.
- ☐ Grated or sliced cheese, tomato or green pepper.
- ☐ Onion rings, raw or fried.
- ☐ Black mushrooms, sliced and fried in butter with just a splash of Worcestershire sauce.
- ☐ Condiments like relish, pickles, mustard, chutney, tomato sauce.
- ☐ Crisply fried bacon bits, or egg and bacon fried in a pan over the coals.
- ☐ A scattering of fresh sprouts.
- ☐ Fresh watercress or coriander sprigs.
- ☐ Mashed avocado seasoned with salt and milled pepper and lemon.
- ☐ Blue cheese whizzed with cream cheese and a touch of olive oil, lemon juice, freshly milled black pepper and a handful of nuts for texture.
- ☐ One of the sauces in this book: Herbed Tomato Sauce (page 68), Barbecue Sauce, or Quick Satay Sauce (both page 69).

Indonesian Satay (page 26)

MEAT 27

Parsley-Pasted Venison saddle (page 29), Herbed Orange, Onion and Olive Salad (page 71)

VENISON

South Africans are lucky to have a fair supply of venison, either from hunting relatives, friendly farmers or specialist butchers. The finest flesh comes from animals under two years old, the most tender cuts coming from the haunch, loin and saddle. These may be left whole or sliced into chops or steaks.

Venison tends to be dry and, if unmatured, fairly tough. The usual maturing process is to gut and hang it without removing the skin, in a cool room for between 1 and 3 weeks. The ideal temperature is 3-5 °C.

Marinating also tenderises venison. Large cuts should be marinated for several days, smaller chops and steak for 4-5 hours. Use one of the marinades starting on page 22, or plain buttermilk if you prefer. However, there's no need to marinate young game as the delicate flavour will be spoilt. Simply brush with oil or flavoured butter.

Larding adds moisture to the very fibres of the meat. Use lard, spek or streaky bacon cut into strips. Use a larding needle and insert slivers of fat with the grain of the meat. Afterwards cut the meat into chops or steaks.

Barding – merely covering the meat with a layer of spek or bacon, tied into position with string – is another way of adding succulence to venison. Traditionalists would never use anything other than a sheet of caul fat. This is the fine, lacy fat surrounding the stomach and entrails of pigs, sheep and game. It sticks to the meat and gradually melts, basting and adding flavour in the process.

A real hunter's treat is the marrow from the shinbone of larger buck such as gemsbok or kudu. Simply toss the bones into the coals for 30 minutes (longer if you like – it won't overcook), then tap off the ashes and chop the bones open to extricate the tasty, tender marrow. Serve on just-braaied toast or nestled in a baked potato.

The recipes that follow are specially for venison but many of the beef and lamb recipes can be used too.

PARSLEY-PASTED VENISON

Braai a chunk of venison moistened with a fresh parsley and butter mixture – and carve it into thick steaks afterwards.

1,5-2 kg whole venison steak
  (rump or fillet)
salt and milled black pepper

PARSLEY PASTE
50 g (50 ml) soft butter
45 ml chopped parsley
  (don't substitute dried parsley)
3-4 cloves garlic, crushed
milled black pepper

Mix all the ingredients for the parsley paste. Reserve half for a basting sauce. Make small incisions in the meat here and there and fill them with little dabs of the parsley paste. Heat the remaining mixture just enough to melt the butter and use to baste while braaiing.

Season meat with salt and pepper and brown well over hot coals, turning to seal on all sides. Cook until medium done inside, basting frequently. An internal temperature of 60 °C on a meat thermometer is just about right.

Allow the steaks to rest in a warm spot for 5-10 minutes before carving into thick slices. Drizzle over any remaining parsley butter and serve with a sauce of your choice.
Serves 6-8

BONED LEG OF VENISON

Young, small game are best in this recipe. These include springbok, steenbok, impala, ribbok, bosbok, blesbok and duiker.

1 leg of venison
6 cloves garlic, peeled and slivered
100 g rindless streaky bacon for
  larding, cut into small pieces
Seven Spice Mix
  or Roasted Braai Spice
  (both recipes page 22)
large piece of caul fat
  or melted butter
salt

With a sharp knife, cut along the leg bone. Remove the bone, lay the meat flat and make incisions in it to achieve a more or less uniform thickness. Make small incisions in which to press garlic slivers and bacon bits. Dust with spice mixture and wrap in caul fat.

Braai over medium coals, turning regularly and basting with melted butter if you haven't used caul fat. Cooking time is about 30 minutes depending on the size of the leg and how well done it must be. Leave it in a warm spot for about 10 minutes to rest before carving.

Remove caul fat and carve meat into thick slices. Season with a little salt and serve with a potato side dish and a sauce of your choice.
Serves 8-10

MEAT 29

Loin of Lamb with Garlic and Rosemary (page 31), served with Ratatouille (page 81) and Coal-Roasted Garlic (page 78)

LAMB

Many memorable feasts spring to mind when thinking of braaied lamb – whole spitroast sheep, succulent chops, crisp ribbetjies, butterflied legs, tender loins and spicy sosaties.

The tenderness of lamb improves with maturing. Choose large cuts with a good fat covering (not chops – they'll dry out), wipe with vinegared cloth and place uncovered on a fridge shelf for 2-5 days.

The most popular cuts for braaiing are from the rib or loin (cut into chops or left as a whole saddle), leg (whole, boned or cut into chops), thick rib, chump (which yields the best chops), or a whole shoulder which should be braaied very slowly over coolish coals.

Choose chops that are cut fairly thick – about 2 cm is perfect. Thinner chops dry out miserably over the coals. Slash the fat at intervals to prevent them from curling up as they cook, and season just before cooking or after browning. Lamb is happy teamed up with herbs, so have fun experimenting with your particular favourites. Lamb also marinates well. Aim for meat which, when about to be served, is still pink. It'll be far more tender, succulent and flavoursome than well-done lamb can ever be.

MINTY CHOPS

A hint of mint elevates lamb to new heights and is used here as an integral part of a piquant marinade. Use any type of chop.

6-8 lamb chops, cut nice and thick
salt and milled black pepper

MINT MARINADE
60 ml mint jelly
15 ml chopped mint
   or 5 ml dried mint
30 ml sunflower or olive oil
squeeze of lemon juice

TO SERVE
mint jelly

Mix marinade ingredients in a saucepan and warm to melt jelly. Pour over chops, cover and marinate in the fridge for several hours – overnight if you wish.

Season chops lightly with salt and pepper and braai over hot coals for 3-5 minutes each side depending on thickness – the meat should still be pink inside. Baste frequently with the marinade while cooking.

Garnish with fresh mint sprigs and serve at once with extra mint jelly.
Serves 4-6

LOIN OF LAMB WITH GARLIC AND ROSEMARY

A spectacular dish that cooks perfectly on an open grid or under the cover of a dome.

1 whole loin of lamb
   (allow 1-3 chops per person)
slivers of garlic
sprigs of rosemary
salt and milled black pepper
olive or sunflower oil for basting

Let your butcher cut through the bones for easier carving. Insert slivers of garlic into the fleshy part of each chop and pack a generous sprig of rosemary between each one. Season meat with salt and pepper.

Brown well over hot coals, then cook over a more moderate heat, turning the rack this way and that until it's done to the desired degree – 50-60 minutes' cooking time should be sufficient for a nice plump piece of meat. Allow less time for a leaner joint with smaller chops. An internal temperature of 65-70 °C should be just right.

It is permitted and often preferable to carve on the grid, so the tastes of all guests can be catered for; those who prefer pink lamb may be served first while those with a penchant for burnt offerings can wait a while longer.

BUTTERFLIED LAMB

For a special treat, bone a leg of lamb (see page 32) and cook to succulent perfection with a crispy charcoaled outer layer.

2 kg leg of lamb, boned
   (about 1,5 kg boneless meat)
salt and milled black pepper
sunflower oil

ORANGE AND ROSEMARY BASTE
125 ml olive oil
125 ml dry white wine
grated rind and juice of 1 orange
2 cloves garlic, crushed
30 ml rosemary needles
   or 10 ml dried rosemary
30 ml chopped parsley
   or 10 ml dried parsley

Score the fat with a criss-cross pattern and season the meat with salt and pepper. Heat the grid and brush with oil. Lightly oil the lamb, too, to prevent it from sticking. Mix all the baste ingredients together.

Brown the joint over hot coals to seal all over. Baste liberally, then raise the grid from the heat to cook the lamb over a more moderate heat. Ensure that the cooking speed is maintained by augmenting the coals, or by lowering the grid as the coals die down. Continue to turn and baste the meat frequently as it cooks, which will take 50-60 minutes. You'll be sure of the degree of done-ness by using a meat thermometer. An internal temperature of 65-70 °C means medium-cooked meat – still rosy within the thicker parts. Cook a while longer if you prefer it well done.

Allow the meat to rest in a warm spot for about 10 minutes before carving, across the grain, into thick slices. Garnish with sprigs of rosemary.
Serves 6-8

VARIATION
Instead of basting your lamb, glaze it after braaiing. See recipe on page 32.

APRICOT GLAZE

400 g tin apricots, drained
   (reserve syrup)
60 ml apricot syrup (from the tin)
60 ml olive oil
30 ml chopped mint
   or 10 ml dried mint
2 ml salt
milled black pepper

Whiz the ingredients in a food processor until velvety smooth. Use to brush the lamb as it cooks.

BONING A LEG OF LAMB

A boneless piece of meat means easier carving and also allows quicker cooking of joints more suited to oven roasting – especially if you cook it under a hood, where the heat is trapped and circulated round the joint and cooks it from all sides.

Boning a leg is really quite simple, especially if it's well chilled. Your butcher will happily do it for you. If not, here's how to do it yourself:
A shortish, razor-sharp knife is essential. Choose one with a pointy tip and a firm, narrow blade. Start boning where the bones are visible, working with short movements, scraping away the meat from the bones.
1 Cut off the shank from the rest of the leg.
2 Remove pelvic bone, starting from the chump end.
3 To remove marrow bone cut through the meat covering the bone, scrape away the surrounding meat, and pull out the bone.

ROLLED LAMB WITH PINEAPPLE STUFFING

A festive dish, and one that requires patience and coals aplenty. Cooking under a hood is desirable, though not essential.

2,5 kg leg of lamb, boned
   (2 kg boneless meat)
salt and milled black pepper

PINEAPPLE STUFFING
1 small onion, finely chopped
30 g (30 ml) butter
400 g tin crushed pineapple,
   well drained
   (reserve syrup for the baste)
250 ml fresh breadcrumbs
30 ml chopped herbs (parsley,
   thyme, marjoram)
   or 5 ml dried mixed herbs
2 ml salt
milled black pepper

PINEAPPLE BASTE
syrup from tin of crushed pineapple
50 g (50 ml) butter

Soften onion in butter in a medium saucepan, then mix with remaining stuffing ingredients.
Lay the boned lamb flat and season with salt and pepper. Spread on the stuffing, roll up and tie securely with string at intervals of about 5 cm.
Combine basting ingredients in a small saucepan and heat to melt the butter.
Brown the meat on all sides, then cook over more gentle coals until done and an internal temperature of 65-70 °C is reached. Baste occasionally.
Allow the meat to rest for 10 minutes before carving into thick slices.
Serves 8-10

SIAMESE SATAY

Tender skewered meat with a strong eastern influence, Siamese satay is rather less spicy than Indonesian satay.

1 kg lean, boneless lamb, chicken, pork or veal

SIAMESE MARINADE
250 ml coconut milk *
30 ml ground almonds
5 ml crushed green ginger
   or 2 ml ground ginger
5 ml ground coriander
5 ml ground turmeric
5 ml sugar
5 ml salt
milled black pepper

* Available tinned or powdered. Alternatively, blend 200 ml desiccated coconut in 300 ml hot water in a food processor or blender, then strain.

Trim meat and cut across the grain into thin slivers about 5 mm thick. This is easiest to do if the meat is semi-frozen. Mix all marinade ingredients and toss meat in mixture until well coated. Cover and set aside in a cool spot or in the fridge for a couple of hours to marinate. If you wish, do this up to 8 hours ahead.
Fold meat evenly and thread onto thin bamboo skewers, forming tightly packed, even kebabs. Braai over hot coals for 10-15 minutes, turning frequently to ensure even browning. Serve with Quick Satay Sauce (page 69).
Makes 6-8 kebabs

SHISH KEBABS

This spicy recipe is as true as possible to the original Turkish one, though now that refrigeration has removed the necessity of spicing as a means of preservation, latter-day kebabs have a more gentle flavouring.

1 kg lean, boneless lamb, from loin
   or leg
16 cocktail tomatoes
16 button mushrooms
2 green peppers cut into chunks

32 MEAT

MARINADE

60 ml olive oil
60 ml wine vinegar
125 ml dry white wine
3 cloves garlic, crushed
3 cm stick cinnamon, crumbled
1 bay leaf
1 sprig tarragon
  or 5 ml dried tarragon
1 ml mustard seed
1 ml ground allspice
1 ml ground coriander
1 ml ground ginger
salt and milled black pepper

Mix all marinade ingredients together, then cut meat into small, even cubes and toss in the mixture to coat. Cover and refrigerate for 24-48 hours, turning the meat occasionally.

Drain meat, reserving the marinade to use as a basting sauce, and thread onto 8 skewers with tomatoes, mushrooms and chunks of green pepper.

Braai over medium-hot coals for about 20-25 minutes, basting and turning occasionally. Serve with rice.
Serves 8

SOSATIES

Tender, tangy and the soul of a braai – South Africa's answer to the Turks' shish kebabs, and equally seductive.

1 large leg of lamb (about 2,5 kg),
   boned, trimmed and cubed
125 g dried apricots
sheeps' fat or sliced bacon

MARINADE

2 large onions, skinned and quartered
125 ml white vinegar
375 ml dry red wine
12 lemon leaves, bruised for flavour
15 ml brown sugar
45 ml curry powder
30 ml ground coriander
10 ml salt
5 ml ground allspice
2 ml ground cinnamon
2 ml ground cumin
1 ml ground cardamom
milled black pepper

In a medium saucepan combine marinade ingredients, cover and simmer for 5 minutes. Cool, then pour over cubed lamb, turning to coat well. (Use an enamel, glass or stainless steel container.) Marinate, covered and refrigerated, for 3-5 days, turning the meat a couple of times a day.

Before preparing the skewers place dried apricots in a small bowl, pour over boiling water and leave to plump for an hour or two.

Assemble the sosaties like this: cut the fat into the thinnest slivers possible, then thread with the meat, apricots and slices of onion (from the marinade) onto the skewers. Return sosaties to the marinade until braai time.

Braai over hot coals, basting with remaining marinade, for 15-20 minutes. The lamb should still be pink and moist in the centre.
Makes about 16

WATCHPOINTS
☐ Fat slivers alongside the cubes of meat impart essential moisture to the meat. Fat trimmed from sheeps' kidneys is best but thinly-sliced, fatty bacon may be substituted.
☐ A long marinating period is essential for a true sosatie flavour.
☐ Overcooking will ruin them!

MAKE AHEAD
Sosaties freeze well but do so after marinating. The curry flavour deteriorates after 8 weeks.

SOUTRIBBETJIES

Crisply braaied lamb ribs are a much-loved traditional dish. Some maintain that the rib should be parboiled to reduce the braaiing time and make it more tender. This method does save time, but there is a loss of flavour.

1,5-2 kg rib of lamb, in one piece
15 ml whole coriander
60 ml coarse salt
10 ml brown sugar
2 ml saltpetre

Trim ribbetjie of excess fat and slash the fat to allow it to cook away.

Roast coriander seeds by tossing them about in a dry, non-stick frying pan until aromatic and lightly browned. Grind finely and mix with salt, sugar and saltpetre. Rub the mixture into the surface of the meat, then hang for several hours to wind-dry in a spot where there's good air circulation.

Soak the meat for 30 minutes in cold water to get rid of excess seasoning. It's now ready for braaiing.

You'll need sufficient coals for about an hour's cooking. Start the process with the meat high above the coals, so it can be heard sizzling very gently and browning only slightly. Bring it nearer the coals as they die down and the result will be tender, crisp morsels to be cut in finger-sized portions. Serve with lemon wedges for squeezing or your favourite sauce to dunk the pieces of rib in.
Serves 4; more if offered as a starter

MEAT 33

Glazed Gammon with Pineapple (page 35)

34 MEAT

PORK

Porkers are slothful creatures which is probably why pork is the tenderest, leanest meat around – there's but little muscle development. Furthermore, improved farming methods and strict health regulations make it absolutely safe to eat so there's no need to overcook it.

Aim for an internal temperature of 75 °C, at which stage it has lost all traces of pink and the meat is at its peak of succulence and flavour. It's not that easy to check the temperature of a chop, so test with a skewer. As soon as the juices run clear, serving time has arrived.

Another option is to braai a whole rib or loin and cut it into chops after about one hour's braaiing, at which point it's easy to see how much more cooking time is required.

For braaiing, choose from the following cuts: rib, loin (whole or cut into chops), fillet, spareribs, chump, thick rib, leg (for kebabs), and neck, which may be braaied whole or cut into steaks. Don't slice your chops too thin, or the meat may dry out – 2 cm is the ideal thickness.

Season well before braaiing and rub the rind with salt for crispiest results. Pork takes well to marinating and basting, which also protects the flesh from the drying effects of the fire.

Coals should ideally be medium to cool for pork. Lower the grid close to the heat at the end of the cooking time to add crispness and character. Serve with a fruity garnish to add flavour.

DIJON PORK STEAKS

Slice boneless pork neck for this recipe; the meat is well marbled and braais beautifully. Alternatively use boneless pork chops.

6-8 thick pork steaks
salt and milled black pepper
ground cumin
30 ml Dijon mustard
30 ml brown sugar

Trim steaks and season with salt, pepper and cumin. Mix together mustard and sugar and reserve.

Braai steaks over medium coals until crisp and just cooked through. A few minutes before the end of the cooking time smear the mustard mixture on each and allow it to heat through and become bubbly. Don't turn the meat again or you'll lose the lovely topping in the coals! Serve at once.
Serves 4-6

PORK WITH MINTED APPLE

Pork and apple are synonymous and this recipe gives a new slant to a very successful flavour combination.

4 pork cutlets or steaks, about 2 cm thick
salt and milled black pepper
2 Granny Smith apples
15 ml chopped mint
 or 5 ml dried mint
60 ml Calvados, brandy, cider
 or apple juice

Trim meat and season with salt and pepper. Peel, core and slice apple thinly. In the centre of four squares of buttered heavy foil place half of the apple and half the mint. Position cutlets or steaks on top and finish all with remaining apple and mint. Drizzle over Calvados, brandy, cider or apple juice and seal the parcels.

Cook on the grid over medium coals for 20-30 minutes until cooked through. It isn't necessary to turn the parcels, as the heat trapped within cooks from all sides. Serve directly from the foil parcels.
Serves 4

MAKE AHEAD
Parcels may be prepared, sealed and refrigerated up to 24 hours ahead of time.

GLAZED GAMMON WITH PINEAPPLE

Smoked gammon steaks, Kasseler chops or gammon roll steaks are all perfect in this recipe which is an all-time favourite.

8 thick gammon steaks
8 slices fresh or tinned pineapple
8 maraschino cherries (optional)

SPICED HONEY GLAZE
60 ml honey
15 ml brown sugar *
30 ml vinegar
15 ml lemon juice
2 ml ground allspice
5 ml cornflour
30 ml soy sauce

* If using tinned pineapple replace sugar with syrup from the tin

Combine glaze ingredients in a small saucepan and bring to the boil, stirring. Simmer for a minute or so until clear and thickened. Allow to cool.

Dunk gammon and pineapple into the glaze before braaiing and baste while cooking as well. Neither gammon nor pineapple require lengthy cooking, but make sure they are well browned.

To serve, top each slice of meat with a piece of pineapple garnished with a cherry and add a sprig of mint if it's handy. Heat the remaining glaze and offer as a separate sauce.
Serves 8

MEAT 35

PORK FILLET WITH BACON AND BANANA

Parcelling in bacon and banana keeps pork moist while braaiing. The procedure isn't as precarious as it sounds and you'll be rewarded with tender meat and a fruity sauce trapped in a crisp layer of bacon.

1 pork fillet, trimmed
salt and milled black pepper
Dijon, French or coarse mustard
3-4 rashers rindless streaky bacon
1 banana, mashed

Season pork with salt and pepper and spread lightly with mustard. Lay down strips of bacon, the pieces slightly overlapping, until there is sufficient to accommodate the pork fillet. Spread mashed banana on the bacon. Lay the fillet on top, then roll up and secure with toothpicks. Place in the freezer for about 30 minutes to firm up or refrigerate overnight if you prefer.

Braai over medium coals until pork is cooked through and bacon crisp. Handle with care and turn as infrequently as possible until the bacon crisps up. Cooking time should be about 20-30 minutes depending on the girth of the meat. To be sure, remove from the grid and cut in half. If there's still a trace of pink, braai for a few minutes longer.
Serves 1-2

VARIATION
Boneless, skinless chicken breasts are equally delicious in this recipe and only take about 20 minutes to cook.

SPICED PORK LOIN

Pork loin is easy to bone and it cooks more quickly too. First scrape the rib bones to allow ends to be lifted from underneath and around the bones. Trim the meat and you're ready to proceed.

1,5-2 kg pork loin, boned, trimmed
salt
Roasted Braai Spice (page 22)

Rub meat all over with salt and braai spice, place in a plastic bag and refrigerate for 1-2 days. Turn occasionally to coat meat with the seasoning.

Wipe off spices, pat meat dry, and braai over medium-low coals until not a trace of pink is visible – about 1½-2 hours. The internal temperature should reach 75 °C, or test with a skewer. The juices should run clear.

Towards the end of the cooking process, turn the meat onto the rind to toast it for crispy crackling. Don't let it burn.

If you're worried about how the meat is faring, cut it into slices after an hour and complete the cooking like that. Serve with a fruity side dish or sauce.
Serves 6-8

VARIATION
Dispense with the idea of dry seasoning and marinate the joint instead. Recipes start on page 22.

CHINESE SPARERIBS

Pork, lamb or beef ribs are heavenly in this flavourful marinade.

1 kg pork, lamb or beef ribs

CHINESE MARINADE
60 ml soy sauce
30 ml wine vinegar
30 ml dry sherry
15 ml honey
30 ml hoisin sauce *
60 ml chicken stock
5 ml crushed green ginger
   or 2 ml dried ginger
5 ml chopped garlic
   or 2 ml garlic flakes
5 ml five-spice powder **

* No hoisin sauce? Substitute chutney and a pinch of cayenne pepper or chilli powder
** Substitute allspice

Mix all the marinade ingredients together, cut ribs into serving portions, place in a non-metallic dish and pour marinade over. Cover and marinate for at least 3 hours at room temperature or for 6 hours in the fridge.

Braaiing time is about 1 hour; cook at low temperature, with ribs sizzling softly as far as possible from the coals. Bring closer to the heat for the final 15 minutes or so to crisp.

Serve with a bowl of hoisin sauce or leftover marinade for dunking. Thicken it, if you wish, by boiling up with 10 ml cornflour mixed in a little cold water.
Serves 4; more if offering as a starter

PORK KEBABS WITH ORANGE AND BRANDY BASTE

Pork with orange and a wonderfully boozy marinade and basting sauce. Herbed Orange, Onion and Olive Salad (page 71) is an excellent accompaniment.

2 pork fillets, trimmed
salt and milled black pepper
ground cumin
2 oranges

ORANGE AND BRANDY BASTE
grated rind and juice of 1 orange
grated rind and juice of 1 lemon
60 ml brandy
60 ml sunflower or olive oil
15 ml finely snipped chives

Cut pork into smallish cubes and season with salt, pepper and ground cumin. Peel oranges and slice very thinly. Enfold pork pieces in slices of orange or pack them in between and thread onto thin bamboo skewers. Lay in a non-metallic dish.

Combine baste ingredients, pour over the kebabs and set aside in a cool spot for an hour or two. If you prefer, refrigerate for up to 24 hours.

Braai kebabs over hot coals – they should cook as quickly as possible for maximum character and flavour. Use the remaining marinade to baste occasionally while cooking.
Serves 4

VARIATION
If you don't wish to resort to wrapping the pork in orange, feel free to dispense with this part of the proceedings.

Chinese Spareribs (page 36) served with Oriental Noodle and Nut Salad (page 73)

Schnitzels with Ham and Cheese (page 39) served with Charred Vegetables (page 74)

38 MEAT

VEAL

Veal – meat from a young calf – is subtly flavoured and finely textured. It is lean, tender and tends to be dry due to the minimal amount of fat present. For this reason, it's a great choice for kilojoule-watchers and for those whose cholesterol levels are cause for caution.

Take care when buying veal – you may be offered 'baby beef' which is coarser in texture and darker in colour. Veal ranges from off-white for milk-fed calves, to pale pink for older grass-fed calves.

Rather like pork, veal lacks flavour, but it marries well with flavoursome ingredients and takes kindly to marinating. In the braaiing context many of the notes on pork apply, as do all the pork recipes.

Your choice of sauce and side dishes is an important issue – they should be bold enough to enhance the flavour of the meat, yet not so powerful as to steal the limelight completely.

CUTLETS WITH PEPPERED MUSHROOM SAUCE

Veal or pork cutlets cooked in foil with a creamy mushroom and pepper sauce.

4 pork or veal cutlets, about 2 cm thick
salt, milled black pepper, flour
8-10 button mushrooms, sliced
125 ml thick cream
45 ml brandy (optional)
10 ml green peppercorns, lightly crushed
45 ml snipped chives

Trim cutlets, season with salt and pepper, dust with flour and place in the centre of four pieces of buttered heavy foil. Top with sliced mushrooms.

Mix together cream, brandy and peppercorns and spoon a little over each piece of meat. Scatter chives on top and seal well.

Cook on the grid over medium coals for 20-30 minutes. There's no need to turn the parcels as the heat trapped inside cooks from all sides. Serve directly from the foil parcels.
Serves 4

MAKE AHEAD
Prepare and seal parcels up to 24 hours ahead of time. Bring to room temperature before braaiing, or add about 5 minutes to the cooking time.

TARRAGON CHOPS

A great way of treating pork, veal or lamb chops. Apple, Celery and Pecan Salad (page 73) is a good accompaniment.

6 thickish chops
salt and milled black pepper

TARRAGON MARINADE
60 ml apple jelly
10 ml chopped tarragon leaves or 2 ml dried tarragon
30 ml tarragon or wine vinegar
30 g (30 ml) butter

GARNISH
fresh tarragon

Trim chops and lay in a non-metallic dish. Combine marinade ingredients in a small saucepan and heat just long enough to melt the jelly and butter. Allow to cool, then pour over the chops and set aside at room temperature for 3-4 hours, or cover and refrigerate for up to 8 hours if you wish the flavour to come through more strongly.

Season chops with salt and pepper and braai over medium-hot coals for 3-4 minutes on each side – don't overcook them or they'll dry out. As they cook, baste with the marinade.

Drizzle remaining marinade over the chops and garnish with fresh tarragon.
Serves 6

SCHNITZELS WITH HAM AND CHEESE AND HONEYED CURRY BASTE

Veal, pork and lamb schnitzels all work exceptionally well in this recipe – just take special care not to overcook them or they'll be dry and totally unappealing.

6 large schnitzels
6 thin slices Gruyère cheese
6 slices ham
paprika
salt and milled black pepper

HONEYED CURRY BASTE
100 g butter
30 ml honey
squeeze of lemon juice
5 ml curry powder

Flatten schnitzels very slightly by whacking with a mallet. Season on each side with a little paprika and salt and pepper. Lay a slice of cheese and ham on each, fold over and secure with toothpicks to keep them from falling apart.

Combine baste ingredients in a small saucepan and heat gently to melt butter. Mix well and brush over the schnitzels while they cook. Make sure your coals are hot so the meat cooks quickly – about 2-3 minutes on each side.
Serves 6

MAKE AHEAD
The baste may be mixed and the schnitzels readied and refrigerated for up to 8 hours before braaiing.

MEAT 39

Charred Chicken Fillets with Tomato and Coriander Salsa (page 41) served with Pesto Mayonnaise (page 68) and Dirty Rice (page 82)

CHICKEN

Tender chicken trapped in crisp, smoky-braaied skin is an unforgettable mouthful. It's well worth mastering the art of braaiing these birds. Accomplish this by trial and error – and with a few words of friendly advice.

Chicken needs relatively long, slow cooking to ensure that it's cooked within before the outer parts dry out. Do this by reducing the heat after browning: increase the distance between grid and coals, move portions towards the outer edges of the grid or scrape away the coals beneath the meat. Revolve the pieces now and then, check for burning (particularly important with marinated chicken), and cook rather longer on the bony side, which will further protect the flesh from drying out.

Chicken has a built-in fat layer between skin and flesh which melts and lards as it cooks. Hindquarters are fattier than forequarters and more resilient to heat, so take care not to overcook the breasts. They dry out very easily.

Hasten the cooking process without sacrificing too much flavour by par-cooking before braaiing. Depending on the size of the portions, bake at 160 °C for 15-30 minutes or simmer slowly in a marinade or with splash of wine or stock and suitable seasoning. Par-cooked chicken gains in succulence what it loses in braai flavour, as the drying braaiing process is shortened.

When gauging cooking time, experience plays an important part, as the heat of the coals varies so much as does the thickness of the meat. As a quick test, drumsticks of perfectly cooked birds move easily, and juices run clear when the flesh is pierced with a skewer.

To add moisture and flavour – and to protect the meat from the heat – basting and seasoning are very important when braaiing unmarinated chicken. Use melted butter or oil seasoned with a squeeze of lemon or orange juice, salt, pepper and a dash of your favourite spice. Or choose one of the marinades or basting sauces which start on page 22.

CHARRED CHICKEN FILLETS WITH TOMATO AND CORIANDER SALSA

Great for those with a penchant for simplicity and a dash of Cajun flavour.

6-8 boneless, skinless chicken breasts
sesame oil
soy sauce
sea salt and milled black pepper
Fresh Tomato and Coriander Salsa (page 68)

Brush chicken fillets generously with sesame oil and soy sauce. Cook quickly over hot coals; they should be crisp as can be yet succulent within. Be very careful not to overcook them, or the meat will be dry and tasteless.

Remove from the grill, season with salt and pepper and serve at once on a spoonful of salsa. Dirty Rice (page 82) is the ideal side dish.
Serves 4-6

CHEESY CHICKEN IN BACON

A quick and easy recipe that never fails to entrance family and friends. Delicious with sliced tomato with a herby dressing.

8 chicken breast fillets, skinned
milled black pepper
Dijon or coarse mustard
8 narrow slices cheese (Gruyère or mozzarella is best)
about 200 g rindless streaky bacon

Unfold chicken breasts to lie flat, season with a little ground pepper and smear with mustard. Place a slice of cheese inside each and fold chicken over to enclose the cheese.

Wrap each breast in streaky bacon, making sure it's completely enveloped.

Braai chicken over medium-hot coals for 15-20 minutes, turning carefully once, halfway through the cooking time. The bacon will be beautifully crisp and the chicken superbly succulent.
Serves 4-6

VARIATION
Make this recipe slightly simpler by omitting the cheese; it's equally delicious.

MAKE AHEAD
The chicken may be wrapped in bacon ready for braaiing a day ahead of time. Wrap in clingfilm and refrigerate.

ORIENTAL CHICKEN SKEWERS

Shades of the mysterious east impaled on skewers and served as snacks or mains.

6 boneless, skinless chicken breasts
60 ml Ketjap Manis (Indonesian soy sauce)
30 ml sake or dry sherry
2 ml crushed green ginger or 1 ml dried ginger
salt

TO SERVE
extra Ketjap Manis

Cut chicken into strips, place in a bowl and add remaining ingredients. Toss to coat, cover and set aside for an hour or two to marinate or refrigerate overnight.

Thread meat onto thin bamboo skewers, pleating it neatly. Braai quickly over hot coals – 2-3 minutes per side should be sufficient.

Serve straight from the fire with extra Ketjap Manis for dipping.
Serves 6-10

VARIATION
Chunks of chicken livers skewered with the meat make a delicious variation in flavour.

HONEY-GLAZED CHICKEN BREASTS

A delicious, no-fuss method for braaiing moist morsels of chicken in foil.

**8 chicken breast fillets, skinned
salt and white pepper**

GLAZE
**60 ml medium sherry
60 ml honey
20 ml Dijon mustard
40 ml chopped fresh herbs
   or 5 ml dried mixed herbs**

Season chicken with salt and pepper and place in the centre of a square of well-buttered heavy foil. Mix ingredients for glaze, spread over chicken and seal parcels well to prevent moisture escaping.

Cook nestled in medium-hot coals until done – about 15-20 minutes. It isn't necessary to turn the parcels.

Serve the chicken with its tangy sauce directly from the foil.
Serves 4

VARIATIONS
Use different flavourings instead of the glaze. Try chopped banana with a squeeze of lemon juice and a sprinkling of ground cinnamon. Or sprinkle with Parmesan cheese and poppy seeds. Sliced mushrooms are delicious, too. In this case add salt, pepper and a dollop of sour cream.

MAKE AHEAD
Sealed parcels may be stored in the fridge for up to a day ahead of time.

FLAMING CHICKEN

A most impressive dish – boned chicken thighs, subtly marinated and flamed with brandy. In keeping with the image serve with an elegant side dish like Charred Vegetables (page 74) or Garlicky Potato and Onion with Rosemary (page 85).

**8 chicken thighs
salt and milled black pepper
paprika**

SPICY YOGHURT MARINADE
**500 ml plain yoghurt
30 ml brandy
1 small onion, very finely chopped
3 cloves garlic, crushed
5 ml crushed green ginger
   or 2 ml dried ginger
5 ml salt
2 ml ground cumin
1 ml ground coriander
½ ml cayenne pepper**

TO FLAME
45 ml brandy

Bone chicken thighs, working from the underside and gently scraping away all the flesh from the bones. This will allow the innermost parts to gain flavour from the marinade.

Place chicken in a non-metallic dish. Mix all marinade ingredients together and pour over chicken, tossing each piece to coat. Cover and refrigerate for a day, turning chicken once in a while.

Drain chicken and pat dry. Brown over medium-hot coals, then cook at a more moderate rate until done – about 20 minutes. Don't baste while braaiing, or you'll spoil the lovely crisp skin.

Transfer chicken to a warmed serving platter, then warm the brandy over the coals – easy to do in a metal soup ladle. Pour brandy over the chicken, ignite and, as soon as the flames subside, season with salt and pepper and add a little paprika for a dash of colour.
Serves 4-6

VARIATION
Substitute any marinade of your choice for the one above. Recipes page 22.

TUCKERED BABY CHICKENS

With a few clever nips and tucks and a some strategically-placed skewers, the awkward (for braaiing) shape of a fowl can be corrected, enabling it to lie almost flat on the grid.

**2 baby chickens
salt and milled black pepper
paprika
Garlic Butter (page 22)**

Place each bird breast side down on a board and remove backbone, either with poultry shears or by cutting down on either side with a sharp knife. (Toss discarded bits into the stock pot.)

Flip bird over and lie flat. Press down to break the breastbone. To keep the bird prone, pierce with two skewers – one through the wings, another through the thighs. The skewers also provide a useful set of handles with which to turn the birds easily.

Season with salt, pepper and paprika. Brush with garlic butter and braai on an open grid, in a hooded kettle or under a dome of foil to trap the heat and speed up the cooking process. Baste and turn frequently; the chicken should be cooked in about 20-30 minutes. Allow a little longer on an open grid. They are ready when the drumsticks wiggle freely and juices run clear when the flesh is pierced with a skewer.
Serves 4-5

VARIATION
There's no law against larger chickens being braaied in this way, though a hooded braai does the job best as the bird cooks quickly and with the minimum amount of drying out. There's no reason, either, why you shouldn't marinate your chicken instead of simply basting it. Recipes start on page 22.

MAKE AHEAD
Why not have tuckered chickens ready and waiting in the freezer for a last-minute braai? The tedious job of nipping, tucking and preparing will then be out of the way.

42 MEAT

Tuckered Baby Chickens (page 42) served with Garlicky Potato and Onion with Rosemary (page 85)

MEAT 43

Baconed Kidney Kebabs and Liver Over the Coals with Onion (page 45)

44 MEAT

OFFAL

Offal makes an interesting diversion from the usual variety of braaied meats. Kidneys and liver are the most popular and both take on a nice aura of smokiness and extra crispness when braaied. Veal kidneys are pale milky-brown and shaped rather like a bunch of grapes; lamb kidneys are egg-shaped and medium brown with a bluish tinge. If they have to be stored in the fridge for a day or two, keep them in their layer of fat, then braai them encased in this. Slice kidneys in half, cut away the hard, white core, wash well and pat dry. Season lightly with salt and milled pepper and braai for 5-7 minutes just until the last trace of pink disappears.

If you prefer, peel off the fat and skewer them; they certainly look more appetising this way. Raw kidneys are floppy, but have a happy knack of firming up over the heat. Seasoning should be limited to salt and pepper added just before they're placed on the grid, and a brushing of oil to moisten them as they cook and stop them sticking to the grid.

Marinating will ruin the texture of offal, so don't try it. A lick of Worcestershire sauce is delicious, though, added after browning and again just before serving. And serve immediately when cooked; kidneys toughen if kept waiting.

BACONED KIDNEY KEBABS

A complete meal-on-a-stick – kidneys wrapped in bacon and spiked with mushrooms and tomatoes. Prepare up to 8 hours ahead of time and keep well chilled.

8 lambs' kidneys
salt and milled black pepper
cayenne pepper (optional)
16 rashers rindless streaky bacon, halved
16 button mushrooms
16 cocktail tomatoes
Worcestershire sauce

Clean, halve, skin and core kidneys, then cut in half again. Season with salt, pepper and a little cayenne pepper and wrap each piece in a half-slice of bacon. Spike onto slim bamboo or wooden skewers with mushrooms and tomatoes.

Just before braaiing, brush each kebab with Worcestershire sauce and cook over hot coals for about 15 minutes.

Serve immediately; kidneys toughen once cooked.
Serves 4

CHICKEN LIVER KEBABS WITH BACON, PINEAPPLE AND PEPPERS

Serve as a main course or offer as snacks while waiting for the main event.

500 g chicken livers, cleaned and trimmed
butter for cooking
milled black pepper or cayenne pepper
lemon juice
250 g rashers rindless streaky bacon
1 red or green pepper, seeded and cut in chunks
24 chunks fresh pineapple

Cut livers into halves – you'll need about 24 pieces. Brown lightly in sizzling butter (don't cook right through). Remove from the pan and flavour with pepper and lemon juice.

Halve bacon rashers, wrap liver inside and thread onto wooden skewers with pepper and pineapple. Refrigerate for up to 8 hours, then braai over hot coals. It will take about 8-10 minutes for the bacon to crisp and the liver to cook through.
Makes 6 kebabs

MAKE AHEAD
Do so with pleasure, but no longer than 8 hours before braaiing.

LIVER OVER THE COALS WITH ONION

That old favourite – liver and onion – relocates very easily to the braai. Potato and Cottage Cheese Bake (page 84) and Hot Potato Salad (page 85) both make ideal accompaniments.

1 kg calf or lamb livers
olive or sunflower oil
3-4 cloves garlic, finely chopped
salt and milled black pepper
3 onions, sliced
butter and oil for frying

GARNISH
chopped fresh herbs

Trim the liver and remove the surrounding membrane. Cut into thickish slices – about 3-4 cm is about right. Place the liver in a bowl with enough oil to coat lightly, together with garlic and lots of milled black pepper. Set aside.

Fry the sliced onion in butter and oil, or grill over hot coals until golden brown. Keep warm.

Heat a hinged grid until piping hot. Drain liver (don't dry it), clamp it in the grid and braai very quickly over hot coals for about 2 minutes on each side. The outside should be crisply charred and the inside tinged with pink.

Pile the liver onto a serving platter, season with salt, top with onion and garnish generously with fresh herbs.
Serves 6

MAKE AHEAD
The oiled liver may be covered and refrigerated for a couple of hours before braaiing. Turn the meat in the oil occasionally to keep it nice and moist.

MEAT 45

Herbed Pork Sausages and Boerewors (page 47) served with Stywepap (page 61) and Herbed Tomato Sauce (page 68)

46 MEAT

SAUSAGE

Braaied sausage is synonymous with outdoor eating in South Africa, especially if that sausage is boerewors! Competition is keen between aspirant boerewors kings, with wors-mixers going to infinite trouble selecting the right meat, maturing it properly, roasting and grinding the freshest spices and mixing it all in their own special (and secret) way.

Essential equipment is a mincer and filling horn or a mincing attachment to your mixer. Add to this plenty of time and a penchant for messy paws, and you can't go wrong!

If you feel that life is too short to stuff a sausage, there are other types available – just wander into any delicatessen and take your pick. Frankfurters and other smoked sausages need only a cursory introduction to the heat, as the smoking process par-cooks them. Otherwise it's sensible to ensure all sausage is cooked right through, with the exception of boerewors that is home-made or which comes from a reputable butcher who wouldn't dream of adding unmentionables to his mix.

BOEREWORS

Traditional boerewors is a mix of beef and pork suitably spiced, with pungent coriander predominating.

2 kg well-matured beef *
1 kg fatty pork (neck, shoulder, belly)
45 ml whole coriander
5 ml whole cloves
30 ml salt
15 ml milled black pepper
2 ml grated nutmeg
10 ml ground allspice
10 ml brown sugar
125 ml dry red wine or dark vinegar
**90 g thick sausage casings,
  soaked in water**

* *Choose forequarter cuts like chuck or bolo; the fat marbling adds succulence.*

Prepare beef and pork by trimming off all sinew, and other nasty bits and pieces that may affect the texture. To facilitate mincing, cut meat into long, narrow strips about 3 cm in diameter and freeze for about 30 minutes. Mince meat through a coarse mincer for a rough texture, or finely if you prefer. Allow the meat to be fed through with very little assistance from the tamper. Finish by mincing a piece of bread to remove every vestige of meat from the mincer.

Roast coriander and cloves in a dry frying pan, tossing the spices about until uniformly brown and aromatic. Don't let them burn. Grind spices with a pestle and mortar, sift to remove husks, mix with remaining spices and sugar and sprinkle over the mince. Lightly mix in wine or vinegar.

Drain casings and place one end over the filling horn and carefully push all of the casings on leaving a 10 cm length hanging down. Tie a knot in this. Grabbing hold of a second pair of hands at this point makes wors-making less traumatic. You can then feed the mixture in while your friend/lover/boss holds the casings, guiding the filling in.

Feed the mixture into the mincer a little at a time, while securing the casing with gentle pressure of one hand on the horn to control the unrolling of the casing as it is filled. Mould the sausage with your hand to make it uniformly thick. Don't pack the casing too full, or the wors will burst while cooking. And try to avoid air bubbles.

After the casing has been filled, remove it – still attached to the horn – from the machine. Push any remaining boerewors mixture into the casing and tie a knot in the end.

Wors should be braaied quickly, so make sure the coals are good and hot. The skin should be crisp and the middle still slightly pink when the job is done. One last thing: gather your guests round the fire so the wors won't have to wait around before being devoured.
Makes 3,5 kg

MAKE AHEAD
This is one job you won't want to do on the day of the braai – and in any case the wors should mature for a few days for the flavour and tenderness to develop. It can be frozen for up to 3 months, but there will be a definite change in flavour – and not for the better.

HERBED PORK SAUSAGES

The ideal meat-to-fat ratio for pork sausage is 2/3 to 1/3 and the cuts most suited are the neck, shoulder, flank and belly. Your butcher will help you gauge the fattiness of the meat so you may add as much extra fat as necessary. He'll even mince it for you if you ask him nicely!

2 kg pork, coarsely minced
15 ml salt
10 ml milled black pepper
5 ml garlic flakes or powder
2 ml dried origanum
1 ml dried thyme
30 ml dry sherry
**60 g thick sausage casings,
  soaked in water**

Place pork in a large bowl, sprinkle over salt, pepper, garlic, origanum, thyme and sherry and mix well. Fill casings as described for Boerewors (this page).

Divide sausage into 15 cm lengths, tying two pieces of string between each and leaving 2-3 cm of empty casing between each knot to cut sausages.

Braai over medium coals for about 15 minutes. A sample slice should reveal no traces of pink. Nor should you overcook pork sausages – they'll dry out.
Makes 2 kg; 14-16 sausages

MAKE AHEAD
The flavour is developed by placing sausages on the rack of the fridge for 24 hours before cooking.

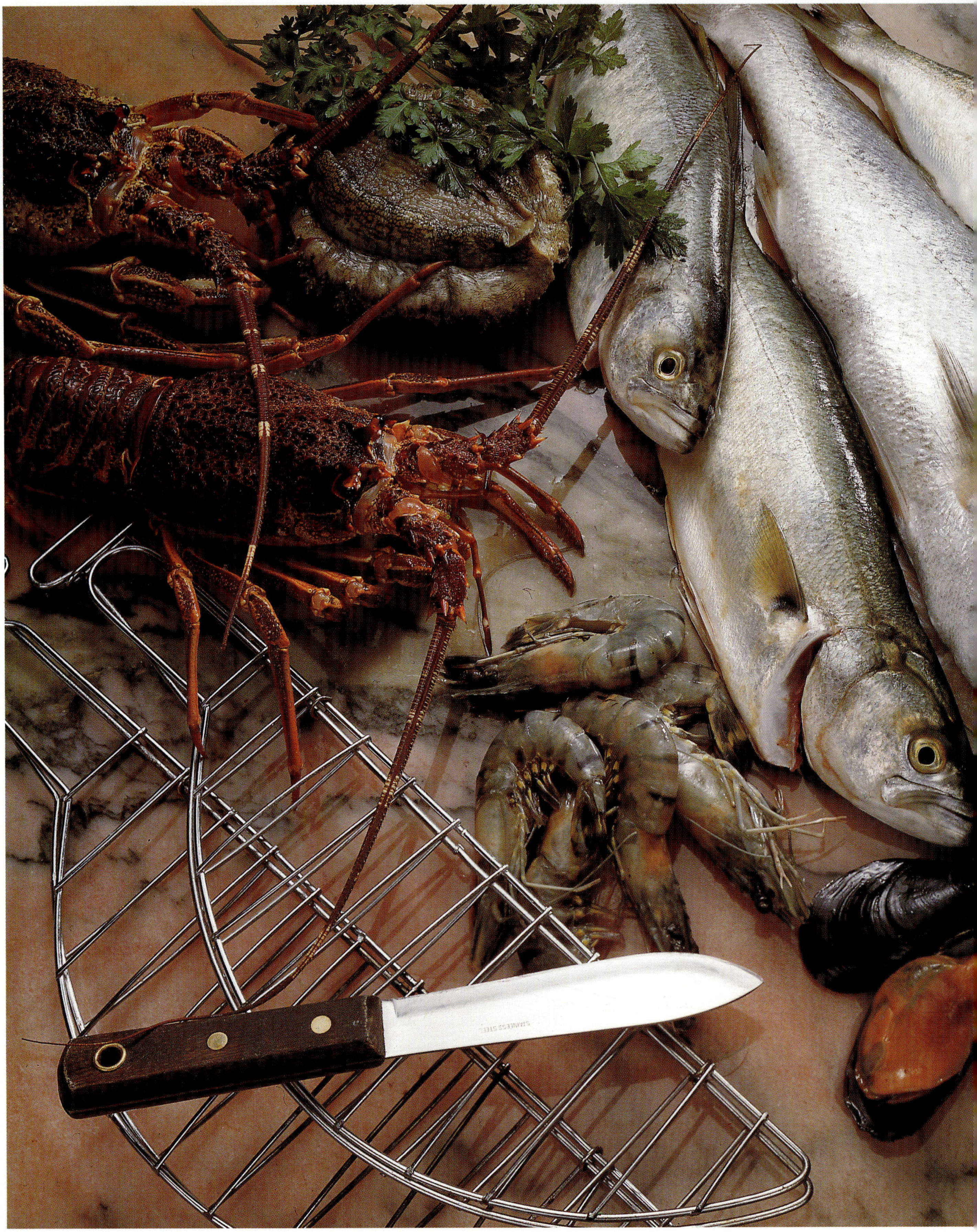

CHAPTER 4

SEAFOOD

For sheer diversity of flavour, little can compare with a seafood braai, especially if the focal point of the meal is a perfect specimen just hauled from the deep. If the braai is on the beach and the anglers or divers are in the gathering, better still, for the sound of the waves, a gentle sea breeze and a few fisherman's tales will make the feast even more idyllic.

Sadly, most of us have to contend with seafood caught by persons unknown, and handled thereafter with varying degrees of care which (mostly) compare badly with the reverent touch that all seafood deserves.

Please remember that specific bag and size limitations apply to many types of fish and shellfish. Before embarking on any seafood-gathering foray, it's a good idea to check the regulations with the Department of Sea Fisheries. They will also advise you if there is any risk of noxious tides affecting seafood.

FISH

Quality is the most important prerequisite for a perfectly braaied fish. Fortunately it's the easiest thing in the world to tell the good from the not so good when it comes to selection. The older the fish, the duller it becomes. Watch for tell-tale signs in the eyes (bright and bulging, not dull and sunken), skin and scales (shiny, bright and moist, not dry and darkened), gills (bright rather than dark) and flesh (firm, moist and odour-free).

Crayfish, perlemoen, elf, kabeljou, black mussels, prawns

Cleaning and storing

When you've selected your fish, decide how you're going to braai it and get your fishmonger to prepare it for you if you're unfamiliar with the procedure. If you're cooking it whole, there are two schools of thought on scaling – those who shudder at the thought of leaving scales on, and those who refuse to remove them, claiming they protect the fish and keep it intact while cooking. Skin and scales can easily be forked away before serving or while eating, so I leave the choice to you.

The fish must, though, be washed and gutted. Then, if you're not braaiing it whole, it may be filleted or cut into steaks or cutlets.

Before braaiing, wrap the fish or fish portions in clingfilm and refrigerate. A really fresh fish may be stored for up to 3 days. Avoid freezing fish at all costs – the flavour and texture will suffer.

Salting and wind-drying

Some fish take kindly to the process of *vlekking*, salting and wind-drying before braaiing. This not only makes the fish more manageable on the grid, but also slightly toughens the outer layer, which, in the heat of the coals, becomes a crisp jacket for the tender flesh within.

Ideal candidates are snoek, yellowtail, harders, elf, galjoen, hottentot, maasbanker and mackerel, although the method may be successfully applied to just about any fish, save the smallest which are bound to dry out, leaving precious little in the way of melt-in-the-mouth flesh.

To *vlek*, cut fish down the belly so that it hinges open at the backbone. Lay it on a tray and salt heavily with coarse salt. Set aside for 30 minutes, then rinse off the salt and salt lightly again with fine salt. Hang the fish on the washing line (or anywhere else out of the cat's reach) for a couple of hours to dry in the wind.

Fish over the coals

Whole or portioned fish may be marinated, basted, foiled or herbed before braaiing, allowing plenty of scope for experiments. Whatever you do, oil both fish and grid beforehand, and heat the grid so that the skin is patterned on contact. A hinged grid is the answer for braaiing fish – it's so much easier to turn.

Never, ever overcook fish; it will dry out and lose most of its flavour and all of its appeal. It's actually easier to braai fish to perfection than to spoil it (unless of course, the poor thing is incinerated), for the flesh is tasty, succulent and tender to start with. It's important to serve braaied fish the moment it comes off the grid. Diners should be ready and waiting, eagerly anticipating the magic moment.

Visual appeal is vital. Serve your fish on a large tray garnished with a profusion of herbs. Lots of lemon wedges are obligatory; thereafter simplicity is the keynote – perhaps a simple salad and crusty loaf or Garlic Bread (page 87). A tasty sauce won't go amiss if you feel like whipping one up (see page 67 for ideas).

Cooking time for fish

Any general rule on cooking time must be tempered with common sense, as the heat of the coals varies, and even the temperature of the fish when placed on the grid affects the timing. So keep checking: as soon as the flesh is opaque it's ready for eating. The well-worn phrase 'when flesh flakes easily' applies as well to fish which is overcooked, so take care on this score.

BRAAIED FISH FILLETS

Purists say the very best braaied flavour is attained when fish flesh and glowing coals get together. This is certainly the way to go for easy serving.

Fillet your fish but leave on the skin. Season just before braaiing, unless you prefer to dry out the flesh a little beforehand. In this case salt the fish heavily, chill for a couple of hours, then rinse, pat dry and season again lightly. Baste fish continually as it cooks, either with a marinade or with a baste of oil, melted butter, or a more elaborate mix of garlic, lemon, herbs and other seasonings.

Quickly brown the flesh side over hot coals, then turn the fish and cook through over a more gentle heat, just until done. Serve pronto with lemon for squeezing. The best types of fish for braaiing in this way are elf, kob, geelbek (Cape salmon), red and white stumpnose, snoek, leervis, yellowtail, musselcracker, red and white steenbras, red stumpnose, dageraad and galjoen.

WHOLE FISH ON THE BRAAI

The very best way to braai a fish is whole – with fins and tail untrimmed – on a grid over open coals. Quite apart from the appearance, an unsurpassed flavour is guaranteed by the flesh gaining full benefit from the smoky heat. Two factors limit this method: the size of the fish and the quality of the flesh. While all but the tiniest tiddler may be safely cooked on the grid, larger specimens may be too big or too thick. In this case a hooded braai or home-made dome of foil comes into its own.

As a general, flexible guide, a whole fish weighing 1,5 kg will take 35-45 minutes to cook.

Favourites for whole-fish braaiing include elf, geelbek (Cape Salmon), dageraad, galjoen, kabeljou, red or white steenbras, musselcracker, roman, red and white stumpnose, seventyfour and silverfish. Smaller species like blacktail, hottentot, bream, fransmadam, grunter and pilchard may also be braaied this way; just reduce the cooking time.

Fish in the lightweight division – 500 g-1 kg braai beautifully with a couple of slashes in their sides. This allows the heat to penetrate quickly to the bone and gives extra flavour. It looks great too. Season the fish with salt, pepper and a brush of lemon juice and olive oil, and fill the cavity with freshly picked herbs to add gentle, herby flavour to the fish.

FISH IN FOIL

Most delicately-fleshed fish is best sealed in foil before braaiing, although the end result may fall somewhat short of the full braai flavour. One way of adding to the flavour is to remove cooked fish from the foil and sizzle it quickly over the coals to brown it before serving.

This cosy method of cooking has the added advantage of retaining the moisture within the foil (unless of course some silly clot pricks it). The juices may be served with the fish or added to the accompanying sauce.

Remember to use heavy foil and to smear it with oil or butter. If you don't there's every chance the fish will stick and look lousy when it's served.

Flavouring foiled fish is a breeze – simply add your favourite goodies to the parcel. Herbs are delicious, as is a squeeze of lemon juice, a dash of wine or a few drops of soy sauce. Vegetables may also be wrapped in the parcel, but remember to slice them evenly so they cook uniformly. In all cases beware of too heavy a hand – it's the flavour of the fish you're after.

Favourites for braaiing in foil include roman, white and red stumpnose, hottentot, musselcracker, dageraad, geelbek (Cape salmon), kabeljou, galjoen, bream, blacktail, zebra and salmon trout. The best, size-wise, weigh less than 2 kg.

PLOUGH DISC FISH

Fish or fish portions may be cooked on a solid metal plate, plough disc or wok over the coals. In this case it's not really braaiing, but frying. The fact that there's a fire beneath is quite coincidental.

To prevent the fish from sticking, butter or oil – or a mixture of both – must be used. All manner of other seasonings may be added: freshly chopped herbs, crushed garlic, lemon juice, dry white wine, beer or a dash of sherry all of which will make a lovely sauce to serve with the fish as long as it hasn't been burnt by cooking over too-fierce heat.

Braaied kabeljou, vlekked elf

SKEWERED TIDDLERS

Impaling the tiniest fish is an ideal way to braai them. Not only are they cooked quickly and easily, but guests never seem to mind plucking out bones as they go. Ideal fish include sardines and harders.

small fish
salt and milled black pepper
olive oil or melted butter

Spike the fish onto skewers, season with salt and pepper and brush with oil or melted butter. Braai until crisp over hot coals and serve straight from the grid for tasty pre-braai snacks.

BLACKENED FISH WITH SPICED CUCUMBER YOGHURT

Cajun spicing adds tantalising flavours to the food scene, in this case succulent fish in a spicy hot crust. Red fish is the choice of traditionalists (stumpnose, steenbras, roman) but other types are also delicious, particularly yellowtail, tuna, angelfish, geelbek (Cape salmon), kabeljou and snoek.

6 filleted fish steaks, each 200-250 g, skin on

CAJUN SPICE MIXTURE
30 ml paprika
15 ml onion salt
15 ml garlic powder
10 ml milled black pepper
10 ml cayenne pepper
10 ml dried origanum
5 ml dried thyme
5 ml ground white pepper

SPICED CUCUMBER YOGHURT
½ English cucumber
salt
175 ml tub plain yoghurt
2 ml Cajun Spice Mixture (recipe above)

Combine all the ingredients for the spice mixture.

SPICED YOGHURT Grate cucumber coarsely, salt lightly and drain in a strainer. Make sure it's really well drained, otherwise the mixture will be sloppy and this will ruin the texture of the sauce. Let it languish in a strainer all day, if you like, then press out excess moisture and combine with yoghurt and spice. Refrigerate until serving time.

Just before you begin braaiing, sprinkle the fish liberally with the spice mixture, pressing it into the surface of the fish to coat fairly evenly.

Make sure that your coals are very hot and braai fish in a hinged grid. The spice will quickly become dark and crusty. You'll ruin the fish if you grip it too tightly in the grid or if you overcook it, so take special care on both counts. First braai the flesh side until it's crisp, then flip fish over and braai the skin side.

Transfer fish to heated plates and place a spoonful of cucumber yoghurt alongside. If you have fresh thyme and origanum available, garnish gaily with a couple of sprigs.
Serves 6

MAKE AHEAD
The Cajun spicing is powerful stuff so coat the fish just before cooking, otherwise the flavour will penetrate the fish and overpower it. Before mixing the spices, make sure they're fresh. Left-over spice may be stored in an airtight jar for several months.

FISH FILLETS WITH MUSHROOMS AND ALMONDS

Mushrooms, almonds and fish – any type you fancy – are perfect partners. Wrap in foil, cook over the coals, and serve straight from the parcels.

4 skinless fish fillets
salt, milled black pepper, flour
60 ml flaked almonds, toasted
8-10 button mushrooms, sliced
60 ml thick cream
30 ml chopped parsley
lemon juice

Season fish well with salt and pepper, dip in flour and place in the centre of pieces of generously buttered heavy foil. Scatter over almonds and sliced mushrooms and add cream, parsley and a squeeze of lemon juice.

Seal parcels well and braai on the grid over medium coals for 15-20 minutes, depending on the thickness of the fish. There's no need to turn the parcels while they cook.

As soon as the fish is opaque (open a parcel to check), serve at once.
Serves 4

MAKE AHEAD
Prepare and seal the parcels, and store in the fridge for no longer than 12 hours ahead of time.

PERLEMOEN

As any lover of perlemoen knows, the flesh of this delicious seafood is fickle stuff, and the pursuit of the perfect steak an all-absorbing pastime. Braaied perlemoen is hard to beat; here's how to go about it.

Preparation
Remove fish from shell, scrub well to remove the greenish film (a pot scourer works well), trim the frilly 'skirt' and clean the dark area where the alimentary canal is situated.

To braai
Slice prepared perlemoen thickly – vertically or horizontally – into thickish steaks, beat lightly to tenderise, season with a little salt, dip in melted butter and place on the grid. Cooking time is minimal – about 2 minutes per side, but the coals must be hot. Serve immediately with a squeeze of lemon.

PERLEMOEN PARCELS

A rather unusual way to prepare perlemoen and one that perfectly preserves its flavour and texture.

perlemoen
butter or olive oil
lemon juice
crushed garlic
milled black pepper
sliced mushrooms
chopped rindless bacon (optional)

Scrub and trim perlemoen – leave them whole – and tenderise all over by beating with a mallet (the outer edges require a great deal more attention than the softer middle part).

Cut pieces of foil large enough to wrap them individually, adding to each parcel a knob of butter or a dash of olive oil, a squeeze of lemon juice, crushed garlic, milled black pepper and some finely sliced mushrooms. Chopped bacon adds a nice flavour variation too.

Wrap securely and braai on the grid over hot coals for 35 minutes. Unwrap and slice the perlemoen and serve with all the goodies from the parcel.

PERLEMOEN IN KELP

This time-honoured recipe results in the tenderest perlemoen, with nothing added to mar the delicate flavour.

perlemoen, cleaned and trimmed
fresh kelp

Slice fairly thickly, tenderise and pack the perlemoen steaks into kelp bulbs freshly cut from the ocean to a length of about 60 cm. Plug the hole with a clean cloth (not a stone; the build-up of steam will simply blast it out), place the operative end in the flames or coals, and cook for 20-30 minutes. Turn only once during the cooking time. To serve, slice a lid off the top of the kelp and tip out the perlemoen and its sauce into a suitable serving dish. Serve with hot crusty bread to mop up the delicious sauce and plenty of well-chilled white wine.

MUSSELS

One of the most addictive braaied treats are freshly-gathered black or white mussels steamed open on the grid and served with a tasty dunking sauce. Try Garlic Butter (page 22), and Vinaigrette or Herb Vinaigrette (both pages 67).

Black mussels cluster on rocks beneath the water and may be gathered at low tide. They grow large enough for a meal-in-one, but smaller specimens are tastier. Scrub shells clean before cooking and soak for a while in fresh water.

White mussels live beneath the sand and are located by twisting bare feet into the sand below the high-water mark. Rinse clean and soak in several changes of water during which procedure much of the sand will be eliminated.

No mussels should be collected from areas polluted by factory or sewerage waste pipes. Neither should they be eaten when affected by noxious tides.

To braai
Before being cooked, mussels must be alive – check by tapping the shell. Jettison those that don't shut pretty smartly. Then place the mussels round the edges of your grid where the heat is gentlest. They'll steam open and are ready for eating straight away. Whatever you do don't leave them on the grid to shrivel and dry out. Pile in a bowl and offer with Garlic Butter (page 22), or sprinkle with Vinaigrette (page 67).

MUSSEL PARCELS

Serve as a starter or accompaniment to braaied fish. Collect and clean mussels as described above, or use tinned mussels. In this case add to the parcels a little dry wine or some of the liquor from the tin to compensate for the lack of natural juices in the shells of the fresh beasties.

18-24 mussels
60 g (60 ml) butter
4-6 cloves garlic, very finely chopped
30 ml chopped parsley
  or 5 ml dried parsley
few drops Tabasco (optional)
milled black pepper

Butter 4 large squares of heavy foil and divide the ingredients between them. Gather up the corners and twist to seal, leaving sufficient space within for the shells to open as they cook.

Place on the grid over medium coals, shaking the parcels gently occasionally to mingle butter, seasoning and mussel juice. As soon as the shells open and everything is sizzly-hot (open a parcel to check), remove from the heat. The parcels may be kept warm round the very edge of the grid for a while, but don't overcook the mussels.

Serve hot with crusty bread to mop up the delicious sauce. Offer salt separately; you'll probably find, though, that fresh mussels have sufficient natural salt to season them.

Serves 4

ALIKREUKELS

Tasty (if a trifle tough) alikreukels are eagerly sought by those spending time on the seashore, gathering them in rock pools at very low tide, or by diving. They are easy to braai, their shells forming the ideal cooking receptacle.

To braai
Simply settle whole, fresh alikreukels, open end up, in medium coals. Soon they'll be bubbling and cooking in their own juices. The moment the 'trap door' attached to the fish can be easily removed (after 20-30 minutes), your snack is ready.

Remove fish from shell, discard the soft, darker stomach part, slice the rest and serve with salt, pepper, lemon juice and a dipping sauce like Garlic Butter (page 22) or Vinaigrette (page 67).

SEAFOOD

CRAYFISH (ROCK LOBSTER)

Some of our most inspired edibles come in forms that probably terrified those intrepid forebears who first shut their eyes, cooked them and changed the course of culinary history forever. And, let's face it, crayfish just aren't pretty. Properly braaied, though, they are one of the world's most addictive delicacies.

Of all perishable goods, crayfish is probably the most vulnerable. Fresh is best and, to connoisseurs, the only way to eat it. Freezing takes its toll on flavour and texture.

When you're lucky enough to come face to face with a fresh crayfish plan a crayfish braai immediately – or at least within a couple of days. During this time your catch will be quite safe in the fridge; the chances are that the creatures will still be wriggling (even if only slightly) after this time.

Preparation
Place on a board, belly down, tail outstretched. Rest a large, sharp knife down the length of the back from the small horn between the eyes. Press down or hit the knife with a mallet to split the shell neatly, then cut through the tail. Open the crayfish, scrape out entrails, rinse and pat dry.

To braai
Season prepared crayfish with salt and pepper, brush with Garlic Butter (page 22) and place, flesh down, on a well oiled grid over medium coals. Cook just long enough to lightly brown the meat, then turn, baste liberally and cook 10-15 minutes further until the flesh is opaque and pulls easily away from the shell.

Serve with a complementary sauce. My favourites include Mayonnaise or a mayonnaise variation, Pesto Mayonnaise, or Fresh Tomato and Coriander Salsa (recipes page 68).

MIXED SEAFOOD PARCELS

Steaming is the perfect way of cooking seafood, and this is exactly what happens when cooking in foil. Combine your favourites from the list below.

strips or chunks of filleted fish
shelled, veined prawns
cubes of crayfish tail meat
perlemoen, sliced paper-thin and lightly beaten
shelled mussels
tiny tubes or rings of calamari
shucked oysters
periwinkles (boil for 5 minutes and extract from their shells)
whole scallops

SEASONING
sea salt and milled black pepper
freshly chopped or dried herbs
lemon juice

Prepare seafood according to type and in similarly-sized pieces as far as possible. Pile into squares of well-buttered heavy foil, season with salt, pepper, herbs and lemon juice and seal well. Cook on the grid over medium coals. Listen to the sizzle – it'll tell you that all's well within and that the tasty morsels are cooking nicely.

Cooking time will depend on the heat of the coals and the size of the portions. Open the parcels after 10-15 minutes to take a peek. Fish should be opaque right through, prawns and crayfish will be pink and opaque. The rest cook extremely quickly, so should be done in time.

VARIATIONS
Add a dollop of thick cream (fresh or sour) and a dash of sherry and paprika before sealing the parcels. Or add an oriental touch with a splash of soy sauce, sweet and sour sauce, hoisin sauce, teriyaki sauce or Ketjap Manis. If a touch of heat turns you on, add a sliced fresh chilli.

MAKE AHEAD
No seafood should hang about waiting for something to happen, so prepare and refrigerate parcels no longer than 8 hours in advance.

PRAWNS AND LANGOUSTINES

As a tasty addition to a seafood braai, or a starter to a meat braai, these delicious shellfish are hard to beat.

Preparation
Prawns and langoustines are normally purchased frozen. Defrost very slowly, preferably in the fridge in a colander set over a bowl. Remove the intestinal thread down the back and, if you prefer, the shell.

To braai
Braai prawns and langoustines on the grid, toss on a solid plate with garlic and butter, or impale on skewers. Serve simply with lemon wedges.

SPIKED GARLIC PRAWNS

These are the ultimate treat for prawn lovers. Langoustines may be substituted, though they take a little longer to cook, around 10-15 minutes in total.

1 kg large prawns, defrosted and cleaned (in their shells)
Garlic Butter (page 22), double quantity

Place the prawns in a non-metallic dish and pour over the garlic butter. Turn to coat evenly, cover and refrigerate for an hour or two – longer if you wish.

Remove prawns from the marinade and spike them onto skewers, allowing a little space between each for the heat to circulate. Braai over hot coals for 6-10 minutes, depending on size, turning and basting frequently.

Heat the remaining garlic butter to serve as a hot sauce, and offer lemon wedges for squeezing.
Serves 4-6

VARIATION
Add a touch of heat to the proceedings – mix a couple of sliced, fresh chillies to the garlic butter or add a dash of chilli powder or masala.

Spiked Garlic Prawns and Braaied Crayfish (page 54), served with Dirty Rice (page 82) and Garlic Butter (page 22)

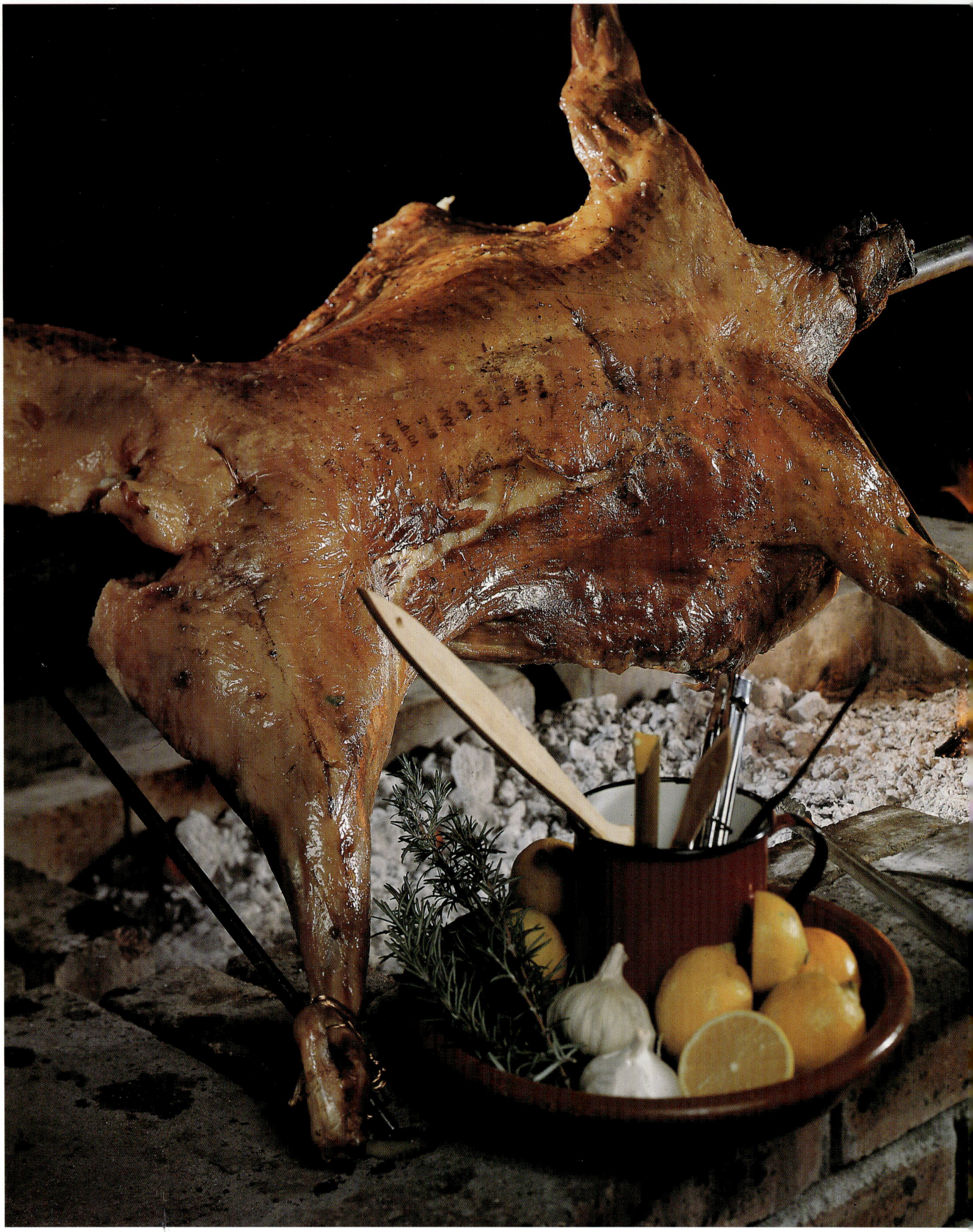

CHAPTER 5

THE SPITROAST

SPIT-ROASTED LAMB

There are several ways of preparing this feast of feasts, all of which involve suspending a whole carcass over the coals and turning it so that it may cook slowly and evenly on all sides.

You'll need:
- [ ] A young, lean lamb – well matured and weighing less than 15 kg.
- [ ] A sturdy spit designed to support the carcass over the coals.
- [ ] A pit in the ground, halved metal drums or a suitable braai area in which to make the fires.
- [ ] Plenty of coals, with reserve fires in the process of burning down to provide sufficient coals for up to 5 hours' cooking time.
- [ ] Interesting conversation and plenty of cold beer to help the time fly by as the lamb is watched, turned, basted and discussed.
- [ ] Many hands and sharp knives to carve and serve the beast.

The spit

Various weird and wonderful contraptions have been dreamed up and, with the exception of the Asado method of spitroasting (see page 58), all require a horizontal bar supported by two uprights. If you're not keen on the meat collapsing into the coals, be sure that all parts of the spit are steady and sturdy.

Spit-roasted lamb

You'll need a horizontal bar on which to secure your lamb with two cross-bars to hold fore- and hind legs. One of these bars may be welded into position, while the other should be left loose to be secured after the lamb is positioned. A handle with which to rotate the carcass must be welded onto the horizontal bar to facilitate turning the beast.

The uprights must stand firmly on the ground and be able to support the lamb-bearing rod at varying heights from the coals to control the cooking speed.

After examining and designing scores of spits, we found the ideal arrangement – a builder's scaffolding trestle. It has two legs, each holding a vertical pipe-within-a-pipe; instant height-varying and spit-holding devices. Increasing the overall length of the trestle is all that's required to accommodate one or two sheep. Here's how: weld in extra lengths of metal in the bars linking the feet of the trestle. Now these feet-linking bars will comfortably hold two metal half-drums in which the fires may be built.

Preparing the carcass

Make sure it's clean: wipe thoroughly with a vinegar-soaked cloth and remove excess fat and unsightly parts.

The legs will be splayed, but there are two ways of handling the rib section. The usual method is to splay it: using a cleaver or axe, partially chop from the inside through the backbone from the neck to between the shoulders, then force the ribs flat. The carcass is now ready to be impaled on the horizontal bar.

Starting at the tail end, lay a supporting rod along the inner side of the backbone and fasten with wire in three places. Secure the hind legs to the fixed cross-bar with wire. Position the loose cross-bar to support the forelegs, fastening it securely to the horizontal bar and the legs to the cross-bar.

Lastly pierce two sharpened green sticks into the portions to be splayed and steadied – the rib section and the flank section. Lay the sticks over the back and into the flesh on either side. If you're worried about your lamb developing a speed-wobble as it cooks, use wire to tie the spine securely to the horizontal bar.

The other way is to leave the rib section intact and use the cavity for seasoning. Rub liberally with salt and pepper and brush with olive oil. Fill the cavity with whole oranges, deeply scored to release their flavour. Handfuls of roughly chopped garlic cloves and fresh rosemary may be added as well. Finally sew the belly closed.

Another idea which adds a real flavour boost is to stud the meat with slivers of garlic and sprigs of rosemary.

Basting and marinating

Some like their lamb to languish for days in a bathful of flavouring mixture, while others permit nothing but a salt and water solution (plus the drippings from the roasting lamb) anywhere near them.

Any of the marinades and basting sauces given in pages 22 to 23 are suitable for lamb, but should be multiplied ten times to provide sufficient liquid.

Cooking time

This is incredibly variable; one can spend twice as long cooking lamb on a cool winter afternoon than in the heat of a high-noon summer – even if a sheet of corrugated iron to reflect the heat towards the meat is pressed into service.

If the weather's hot, allow about 4 hours after the sheep has browned; the juices from the thickest part of the rump should be faintly tinged with pink or should measure an internal temperature of 65-70 °C on a meat thermometer. There will be plenty of well done meat from the ribs and outermost parts to satisfy those who enjoy their lamb like this, and rarer meat on the legs for those who prefer theirs pinkish.

Dining time must needs be flexible. Spit-roasted anything – like a watched pot – simply cannot be hurried along. If your guests start collapsing with hunger, carve off crispy titbits to keep them going until gong-strike.

To carve the beast

The simplest, most efficient way of carving is on the spit. Just lay a grid over the coals, place stainless steel trays on top and raise the carcass away from the heat. The carvings simply drop into the trays and stay nice and warm.

Alternatively do the job on a table. Cover it with plenty of newspaper and sheets of plastic. Large boards placed under the operational areas will help the carvers, and a couple of platters for the carvings will keep things running smoothly. If they're made of stainless steel, so much the better. Lay them on the coolest embers to keep the meat hot while guests help themselves and come back for seconds and thirds.

THE ASADO

Argentina is cattle country, so it's not surprising that the Argentinians have perfected the art of roasting a whole carcass over the coals as their traditional way of entertaining.

The Asado is a method of cooking a whole sheep, secured to a metal spit forced into the ground. The spit holds the carcass at an angle over the coals. As it cooks, fat melts and bastes the meat. The juices may be collected as they drip off and used to baste the meat

The spit

We've tried making this crucifix-type spit in two ways, using both round metal rods and flat ones. The flat rods have several advantages: the sheep is held securely, the rod stays firmly in the ground, it curves slightly to the shape of the carcass and bends beautifully over the coals while supporting the lamb.

Use metal which is 4 cm wide by 6 mm thick. The long rod should measure 1,6 m and the short one 75 cm. The short rod is welded across the long rod about 20 cm from one end to form a cross. Both ends of the main rod are sharpened to easily pierce the carcass – and the ground.

The lamb

Choose a young, lean lamb, well matured and weighing no more than 10 kg. With a cleaver or sharp axe and working from the inside, chop partially through the spine in the area of the ribs. Open and flatten this section, remove and discard the two top chops on either side to allow the heat to penetrate the shoulders, then trim away all extraneous fat and loose skin.

Impaling the lamb

Push the pointed end of the long rod through the flesh from neck to tail, between backbone and skin. Attach hind legs to the cross-bar with wire. Wire also the pieces of flesh between tail and feet to the cross-bar to hold open the leg meat. Slash the leg flesh almost through to the bone on the inner side so the meat cooks evenly.

To hold the carcass open, you'll need three green twigs with pointed ends, similar in length to the cross-bar. Place these across the flank, shoulders and forelegs. Pierce the ends through the flesh to hold it open.

To suspend the lamb over the coals, force the spit well into the ground, just off the vertical, with the lamb's belly towards the heat.

At the start, pile the coals mainly under the legs as these take longer to cook. After 30 minutes or so rake the coals evenly under the lamb. To turn the lamb, pull the rod out of the ground, revolve it and present the opposite side to the heat. The total cooking time will be about 3 hours, when the internal temperature of the leg meat registers 65-70 °C on a meat thermometer, or juices run faintly tinged with pink when the flesh is pierced.

SPIT-ROASTED PIG

A small porker spit-roasted to perfection is a meal to be remembered. Although pork is lean, the fat and rind make it an ideal choice for spit-roasting. As the fat melts it lards the meat, while the rind protects the flesh and becomes crisp crackling at the same time.

Choose a very young animal weighing not more than 12 kg. Depending on side dishes, it'll serve about 24 people. Leave head and tail in situ and splay the carcass ready for roasting as described for lamb. If you'd prefer to keep the porker closed, remove the innards through the stomach leaving ribs attached at the breastbone.

Ask your butcher to score the rind all over in a diamond-pattern. Stuff the piglet with about eight sliced apples and a fistful of fresh mint, then sew up the belly with strong thread or thin string. The cooking fruit and herbs will steam ambrosially, adding moisture and flavour along the way.

Follow the practical instructions for Spit-roasted Lamb, with these variations which apply specifically to pork:

Fasten the carcass very securely to the rod, using thin wire or string approximately hand-spans apart.

Don't marinate pork before spit-roasting, as this may soften the crackling. One may rub dry seasoning into the surfaces, inside and out – Roasted Braai Spice and Seven Spice Mix (recipes page 22) are both ideal for pork.

Cook pork over medium-low coals and watch carefully for signs of burning (crackling-lovers would never forgive you for ruining it). This can always be crisped at the end of the cooking time by lowering the carcass towards the heat, or by sprinkling over a mixture of flour and salt.

Allow longer cooking time for pork than for lamb of a similar size – 4-5 hours may be necessary. As soon as the ribs are well browned, protect them from overcooking by wrapping with foil. This can be removed for the final part of the cooking time which will allow you to crisp them up.

Keep checking the meat for done-ness by piercing the thickest part of the flesh with a skewer. As soon as the juices run clear and an internal temperature of 75 °C has been reached, the pork is ready to be served.

Spit-roasted pig (page 58), served with Glazed Fruit Kebabs (page 92)

THE SPITROAST 59

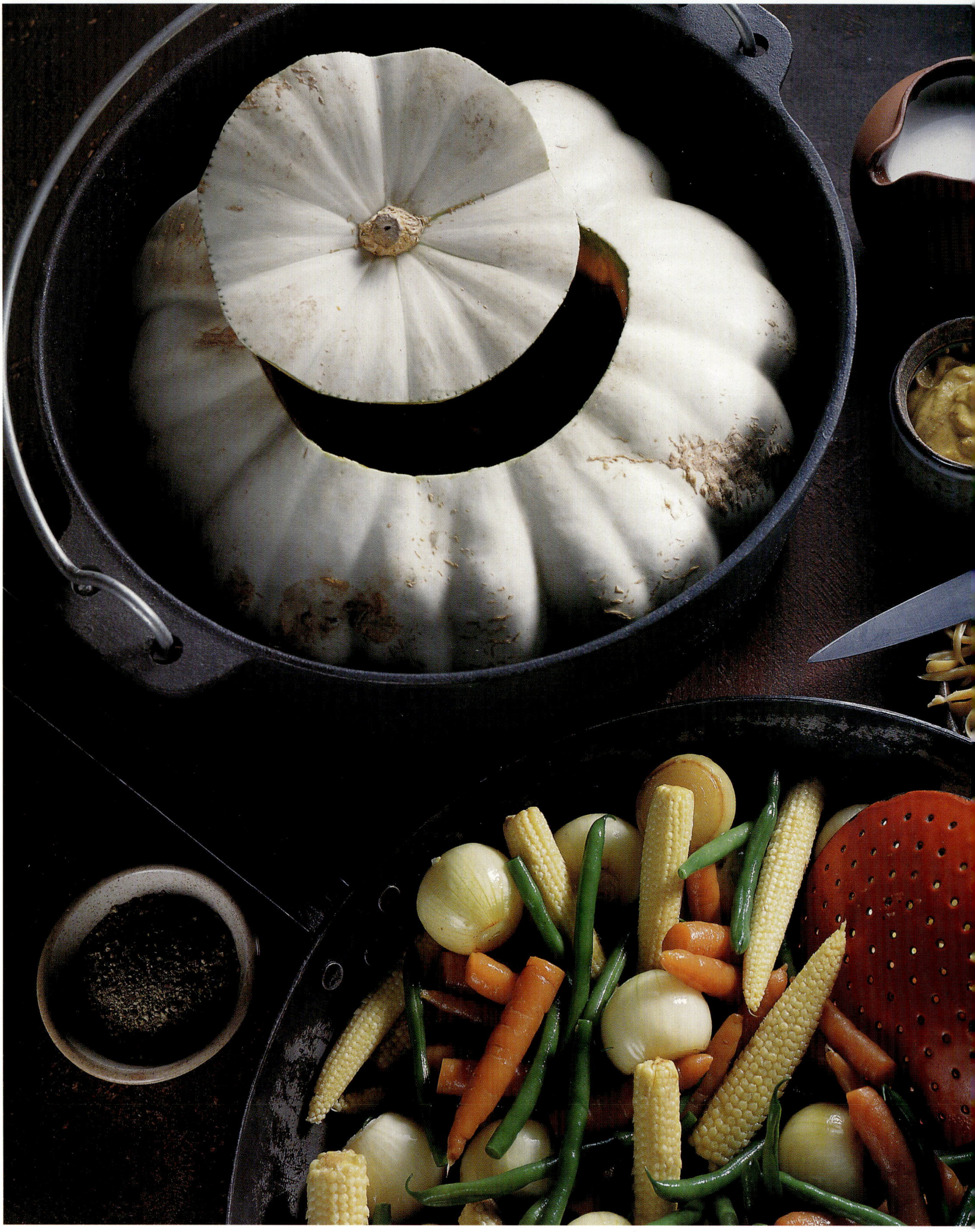

CHAPTER 6

POTJIEKOS

Potjiekos is close to the hearts of outdoor entertainers who are always on the look-out for a way to broaden their repertoire of recipes.

There was a time when potjiekos was all the rage – competitions proliferated and pots were to be found a-simmering in every backyard. Some of the resulting dishes were delicious, others unspeakably bad – which rather dampened the enthusiasm of both potjie-preparers and their guests.

The recipes in this section are a far cry from your average 'layered and never stir it' pot you may be familiar with. Try them. Your potjiekos will never be the same again!

PUMPKIN IN A POTJIE

Fill a scooped-out pumpkin with vegetables, bake it in a potjie and serve as a stunning main or side dish. Any type of pumpkin may be used.

1 smallish pumpkin, about 1,5-2,5 kg
30 g (30 ml) butter
24 pickling onions, skinned
10 cloves garlic
300 g young green beans
300 g baby corn
 or 400 g tin whole kernel corn
300 g tiny carrots
250 ml cream
100 g (250 ml) grated Cheddar cheese
10 ml Dijon mustard
salt and milled black pepper
grated nutmeg

Preparation of Pumpkin in a Potjie

Cut a 'lid' from the top of the pumpkin. Scoop out and discard the pips.

Heat butter in a medium saucepan and sauté onions and garlic until very lightly glazed. Cover, reduce heat and steam until onions are half cooked. Add remaining vegetables (cut corn and carrots in half lengthwise if they are on the large side) and toss about to coat with butter. Add cream, cheese and seasoning and mix well.

Spoon vegetables into the pumpkin, add the sauce, replace the 'lid' and place in a buttered potjie – one just large enough to fit the pumpkin is best. Cook in low coals and place a shovel-full of coals onto the lid as well so the pumpkin bakes from all sides.

Cooking time is about 2 hours. Lift pumpkin from the pot onto a serving dish and slice into wedges.
Serves 8

STYWEPAP

If you're a committed pap-eater, it's hard to imagine a braai without it, especially with Herbed Tomato Sauce (page 68) or Ratatouille (page 81) on the side and nice chunks of braaied boerewors. Prepare it in a potjie over the coals or in a heavy pot on the stovetop. Leftovers may be pressed into flat cakes and fried in butter.

1 litre water
5 ml salt
500 ml coarse mealie meal
30 g (30 ml) butter

Bring water and salt to the boil in a large pot. Add mealie meal all in one go, mix, cover and cook undisturbed over very gentle heat for about 30 minutes. Mix in butter and serve hot.
Serves 4-6

KRUMMELPAP

Also called putupap, this is more crumbly than stywepap, and is usually pressed into small balls and used to mop up the meat juices. Strict traditionalists would never have it with any other sauce.

1 litre water
5 ml salt
750 ml coarse mealie meal
30 g (30 ml) butter

Bring salted water to the boil in your potjie, slowly add mealie meal, stirring constantly. Cover and cook over very low heat for 30-40 minutes, stirring every 10 minutes. Stir in butter just before serving.
Serves 4-6

POTBROOD

In the dim and dusty past, our forebears took bread dough, shaped it into balls and cooked it nestled in the fragrant depths of bredies or in heavy cast-iron pots set in the coolish coals of their campfires.

Potbrood is still popular today, with devotees keeping special pots for this purpose alone.

Use any of the doughs in the section starting on page 87, haul out the potjie and pretty soon the magic aroma of baking bread will pervade the scene of the braai.

Butter the pot very well before plopping in the dough and baking in coolish coals. Pile a spadeful of coals onto the lid to brown and crisp the crust as it cooks.

Alternatively bake the bread in a loaf tin set on a grid to raise it from the base of the pot. This will allow space for a cup or two of boiling water to simmer away underneath – a method which further insulates the bread from the heat. Replace the water every 20 minutes or so; simmering water evaporates quickly, no matter how well the lid of the pot fits. After cooking, crisp the loaf on the grid. The cooking time will vary according to the method used to cook the bread and the heat of the coals – 1-1½ hours should be sufficient for bread cooked over simmering water. Allow less time for bread prepared directly in the potjie. When a metal skewer comes out clean, the bread is cooked. Cool before serving.

MEDITERRANEAN CHICKEN POTJIE

A robust recipe rich with the colours and flavours of the Mediterranean. For a slightly more economical dish, joint a whole chicken and use it instead of thighs.

8-10 chicken thighs
salt, milled black pepper, flour
olive oil
1 large onion, sliced
2-3 cloves garlic, crushed
4 ripe tomatoes, skinned and chopped,
  or 400 g tin tomatoes
65 g tin tomato paste
15 ml vinegar
125 ml dry white wine
125 ml chicken stock
15 ml chopped fresh herbs (basil, thyme, origanum, parsley)
  or 5 ml dried mixed herbs
2 ml sugar
1 red or green pepper, seeded and sliced
10 anchovy fillets, chopped (optional)
16 black olives

GARNISH
lots of freshly chopped parsley

Remove skin and visible fat from chicken, season with salt and pepper and dredge with flour. Heat a little olive oil in the potjie and brown a few pieces at a time. Set browned chicken aside.

Sauté onion and garlic in remaining oil (add a little more if necessary), then stir in tomatoes, tomato paste, vinegar, wine, stock, herbs and sugar. Nestle chicken into the sauce, cover and cook gently for about 45 minutes until cooked. Add sliced peppers and olives 10 minutes before the end of the cooking time.

If you wish to thicken the sauce, transfer chicken and vegetables to a warm serving dish and mix 5-10 ml flour to a smooth paste with some of the hot sauce. Stir this into the boiling sauce and cook for a couple of minutes, stirring all the while.

Pour sauce over chicken, garnish with chopped parsley and serve with rice or just-cooked pasta and a green salad.
Serves 4-6

MAKE AHEAD
The flavour of this dish improves if it's prepared a day or two ahead. Reheat gently just before serving.

BOOZY CHICKEN POTJIE

There's an enormous amount of cream and booze in this recipe – but it's worth it. The sauce is a knock-out! Your potjie should be small enough to cosset the chicken cosily; if it's on the large size cook two chickens and invite extra guests to the party.

1 plump chicken
salt and milled black pepper
bunch of herbs (bay leaf, parsley, thyme, origanum)
sunflower oil for cooking
2 carrots, finely chopped
1 rib celery, finely chopped
1 onion, finely chopped
250 ml white wine
125 ml dry sherry
125 ml brandy
250 ml cream
15 ml cold butter

Wash chicken, pat dry and season the cavity with salt and pepper. Pop the herbs inside and add a couple of garlic cloves if you wish. Heat a little oil in your potjie and brown the bird on all sides. Don't overdo it; a gentle golden-brown is all you need. Remove chicken from the potjie and stir in the carrot, celery and onion, adding a little more oil if necessary. Cover and 'sweat' the vegetables over low heat for about 5 minutes until they're nice and soft. Whatever you do, don't let them brown.

Meanwhile combine wine, sherry and brandy and heat. Return chicken to the potjie, add the liquid, cover and simmer very gently until the chicken is cooked. This should take about 1¼ hours. Remove chicken from the potjie and keep warm. Strain the broth, pressing on the vegetables to extract all the flavour. Return it to the potjie and boil uncovered until reduced by half. Add cream and continue to reduce and thicken the sauce. Whisk in butter and check seasoning, adding a touch of salt if it's necessary.

To serve, joint the chicken and return it to the potjie, or place on a platter and offer the sauce separately.

Serves 4-5

OLD-FASHIONED GUINEA FOWL POTJIE

A rich potroast for cooler days. If guinea fowl aren't available, substitute a duckling or two small chickens which are equally delicious done this way.

3 guinea fowl
guinea fowl giblets (except the livers)
butter and oil for cooking
250 g rindless streaky bacon, chopped
1 large onion, finely chopped
10-12 cloves garlic, peeled
large bunch of fresh herbs (parsley, thyme, origanum) or a dried bouquet garni
375 ml dry red wine
500 ml chicken stock
salt and milled black pepper

TO FINISH THE SAUCE
200 ml port
45 ml cranberry jelly
300 g button mushrooms, sliced

Trim and halve guinea fowl. In a large potjie cook bacon in a little butter and oil until bacon is quite crisp. Stir in onion and garlic and cook until onion has softened. Lightly brown guinea fowl and giblets in the pot. Add herbs, wine and stock and season lightly with salt and pepper. Cover and potroast very slowly for 2-2½ hours until birds are tender.

Place them on a serving dish. Defat the sauce and, with a slotted spoon, discard all the bits and pieces. Add port, cranberry jelly and mushrooms. Cook for a few minutes until mushrooms are tender. Check seasoning and consistency of sauce, adding water if it's too thick or by boiling uncovered to reduce it if it's too thin. Pour sauce over and around birds and garnish with fresh herbs.

Serves 6

MAKE AHEAD
This potjie tastes even better when made ahead and reheated. It is also easier to defat the sauce when it's cold.

OXTAIL POTJIE

Properly prepared, this leaves all other potjies for dead. The secret lies in very long (as in up to 3 hours) and very slow (as in barely simmering) cooking, whereupon the meat should fall off the bone at the touch of a fork. Finely chopped vegetables cook away to make a flavourful gravy.

1,5 kg oxtail pieces
flour
cooking oil
4-6 cloves garlic, crushed
2 large onions, finely chopped
2 large carrots, finely chopped
2 ribs celery, finely chopped
1 large turnip, finely chopped
1 fresh or dried bouquet garni: bay leaf, thyme, origanum
grated rind and juice of 1 small lemon
5-6 ripe tomatoes, skinned and chopped
or 400 g tin tomatoes
375 ml beef stock
250 ml dry red wine
salt and milled black pepper
20 pickling onions, peeled

Dust oxtail with flour. Heat a little oil in a large potjie and brown meat well on all sides – in batches is the best way. Stir in garlic, vegetables, herbs and lemon rind. Add the chopped tomatoes (with the liquid from the tin), stock and wine. Season with salt and pepper, cover and reduce heat to simmer very slowly for about 2½ hours. Stir occasionally.

Add pickling onions, dunking them under the gravy, and continue cooking slowly until they're done. By this time the meat should be fall-apart tender. Skim off the fat and check the seasoning; add extra salt and pepper if necessary.

If there's some handy, garnish with chopped parsley. Serve the dish with rice or Herbed Potato Fry (page 85).

Serves 6

MAKE AHEAD
Oxtail is even better prepared ahead, then refrigerated. In this case transfer it to a suitable serving dish and reheat in the oven or a microwave oven. Alternatively tip it back into the potjie and heat over the coals.

TURKEY IN A POTJIE WITH SPICY RICE STUFFING

Why spend Christmas indoors when the turkey is so easily (and deliciously) prepared over the coals? Like most things, it's easy when you know how.

1 self-basting turkey, about 3,5 kg, defrosted
oil and butter for cooking
salt and milled black pepper
bunch of fresh herbs
grated rind of 1 orange
250 ml orange juice
250 ml dry white wine
250 ml water

SPICY RICE STUFFING
small bunch of spring onions, finely sliced
100 g mushrooms, finely chopped
2 ribs celery, sliced
50 g (50 ml) butter
60 ml sultanas
1 egg
2 ml ground coriander
2 ml ground cinnamon
2 ml ground ginger
250 ml cooked rice
100 g walnuts, crumbled

STUFFING In a medium saucepan soften the spring onion, mushrooms and celery in butter. Remove from the heat, mix in sultanas, egg, spices, rice and nuts and season to taste with salt and pepper. Stuff the belly and neck cavities and truss turkey ready for cooking.

Heat a large potjie over medium-hot coals, add butter and oil and brown turkey well all over. Pour off excess fat, turn bird onto its back and season with salt and pepper. Tuck fresh herbs around the bird. Mix orange rind and juice, wine and water, pour over and cover. Cook very slowly for about 2 hours, basting occasionally, until the meat feels very tender when a skewer is inserted into a leg joint. Add extra hot water if necessary from time to time.

Discard herbs. Place turkey on a carving board in the centre of a tray and garnish with fresh herbs.

If you're serving it warm, tent with foil while finishing the sauce by whisking in a *beurre manie* (equal quantities of soft butter and flour) and boiling until it thickens. Otherwise allow the turkey to cool, garnish with lots of fresh herbs and serve with condiments and salads.
Serves 8-10

SEAFOOD POTJIE

Once the seafood has been prepared (do this a day ahead if you wish), cooking this pot is very quick. Should you not have on hand all the seafood required, feel free to simplify matters slightly, but make up the mass by increasing the other ingredients. Suitable fish to use include kingklip, angelfish, geelbek (Cape salmon), kabeljou, and red or white steenbras.

1 kg filleted fish
4-5 crayfish tails
400 g large headless prawns
400 g calamari tubes
36 black mussels
    or 900 g tin mussels, drained
60 ml olive oil
2 onions, sliced
4 large, ripe tomatoes, skinned and chopped
    or 400 g tin tomatoes
5 ml crushed garlic
5 ml turmeric
60 ml chopped parsley
    or 10 ml dried parsley
salt and milled black pepper
hot water

Skin fish and cut into large blocks. Vein crayfish and prawns (leave shells on). Cut crayfish into chunks. Clean calamari and slice into rings. Rinse mussels with cold water and, if using fresh mussels, pull out the beard.

Heat potjie over the coals, add oil and sauté onion until lightly browned. Stir in tomato, garlic, turmeric, half the chopped parsley, salt and ground pepper, and moisten with about half a cupful of hot water. Cover and simmer for 5-6 minutes. The cooking speed must be very gentle, so scrape away some of the coals to maintain a gentle heat.

Nestle fish and crayfish into the sauce, cover and simmer for 5-6 minutes until seafood is barely cooked. Add calamari and mussels, immersing them in the sauce (add a little more hot water if necessary). Cover and simmer very gently for 1-2 minutes until mussels open, calamari is opaque right through and meltingly tender and all the seafood is cooked to perfection. Check seasoning, scatter over remaining parsley and serve at once.
Serves 8-10

BEEF POTJIE

Full of flavour and great with rice or a potato dish.

1,5 kg stewing beef
60 ml flour
5 ml paprika
5 ml salt
5 ml milled black pepper
sunflower or olive oil for cooking
2 large onions, roughly chopped
10 ml crushed garlic
150 ml dry red wine
250 ml beef stock
45 ml (70 g tin) tomato paste
1 strip orange zest
2 bay leaves
1 stick cinnamon
6 whole cloves
18-20 small pickling onions

Trim meat and cut into large cubes. Mix together flour, paprika, salt and pepper.

Heat potjie, add oil and brown meat very well. Mix in chopped onions and cook until tender. Then add all remaining ingredients except the pickling onions. Cover and simmer very slowly until meat is nearly tender – about 1½ hours depending on the cut of meat. Add pickling onions and simmer for about 20 minutes more until tender.
Serves 6-8

MAKE AHEAD
Like most casseroles, this one reheats perfectly – and tastes even better after a couple of days as the flavours have had a chance to develop.

Seafood Potjie (page 64)

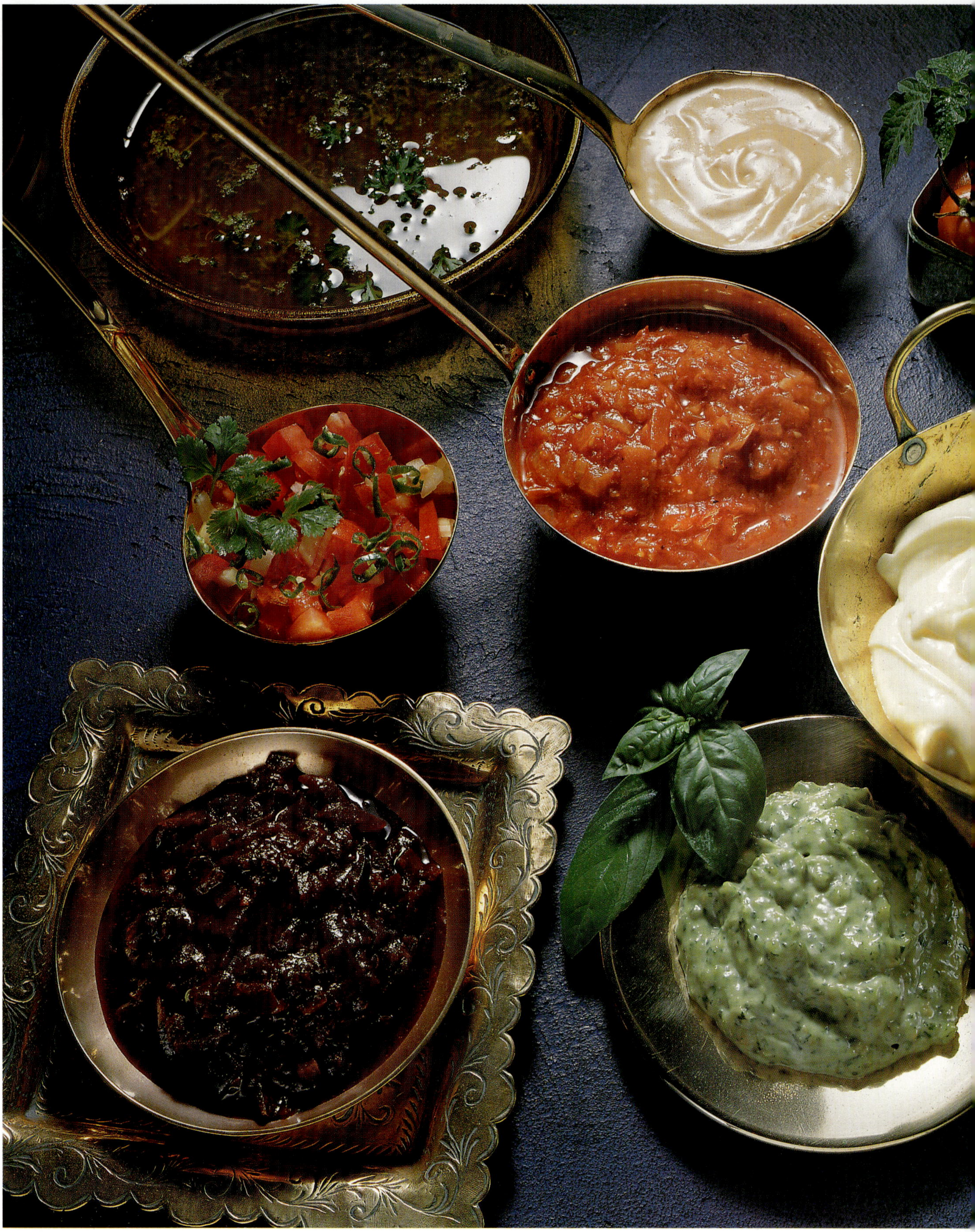

CHAPTER 7

SAUCES AND DRESSINGS

'One who masters the art of sauce-making sits at the apex of the world.' This aptly stresses the importance of a successful sauce in the scheme of things.

A braai is often a quick-fix meal when the family is low on energy and equally lacking in inspiration; a time when a couple of chops and a hastily rustled-up salad will suffice. Summon the enthusiasm to whip up one of these delicious sauces and your reputation will be instantly redeemed.

Most can be prepared well ahead of time, many are quickly made and all will punctuate your catering with the importance of an exclamation mark!

VINAIGRETTE

The classic blend with which to dress a salad. It lasts for weeks in the fridge.

500 ml olive or sunflower oil
   (or mix the two)
125 ml wine vinegar
60 ml lemon juice
2 ml Dijon mustard
2 ml crushed garlic (optional)
2 ml salt
milled black pepper

Blend all ingredients together and store in the fridge. Shake again just before dressing the salad.
Makes 700 ml

Barbecue Sauce, Fresh Tomato and Coriander Salsa, Herb Vinaigrette, Old Man Sauce, Herbed Tomato Sauce, Mayonnaise and Pesto Mayonnaise (pages 67–69)

HERB VINAIGRETTE

This should be freshly prepared, not more than a day ahead.

45 ml olive oil
60 ml wine vinegar
2 ml brown sugar
5 ml Dijon mustard
2 cloves garlic, crushed
6 large mint leaves
   or 2 ml dried mint
30 ml chopped parsley
   or 5 ml dried parsley
leaves from 1 sprig thyme
   or 1 ml dried thyme
salt and milled black pepper

Whiz ingredients together in a blender or food processor, pour into a bottle and refrigerate until required.
Makes about 125 ml

HONEY AND SOY VINAIGRETTE

A mixture of oils adds lovely depth of flavour to this dressing. For extra nuttiness garnish the salad with toasted sesame seeds.

80 ml lemon juice
60 ml sunflower oil
60 ml olive oil
15 ml sesame oil
30 ml soy sauce
30 ml honey

Combine ingredients in a small saucepan and heat very gently – just until honey melts sufficiently to blend with the remaining ingredients. Cool before dressing the salad.
Makes 250 ml

67

MAYONNAISE

This is too useful a sauce not to have on hand at all times – and home-made mayonnaise is so much better than the bought variety. Refrigerated, it keeps well for weeks.

3 whole eggs
2 egg yolks
5 ml dry English mustard
5 ml salt
2 ml white pepper
30 ml white vinegar
30 ml lemon juice
750 ml sunflower oil

In a food processor, blender or electric mixer, whisk whole eggs, yolks, mustard, salt and pepper until pale and thick. With machine running, add vinegar and lemon juice little by little, then pour in oil in a thin, thin stream.

WATCHPOINTS Ensure all ingredients are at room temperature. If you add the oil too quickly or if you add too much oil, the mayonnaise will separate.

Makes 1 litre

VARIATIONS
To 250 ml mayonnaise add …

HERB MAYONNAISE
125 ml finely chopped fresh herbs – choose your particular favourites – parsley, dill, coriander, tarragon, thyme, marjoram, basil, chives

TARTARE SAUCE
2 hard-boiled eggs, finely chopped
15 ml chopped parsley
15 ml snipped chives
  or spring onions
15 ml capers
10 ml Dijon mustard

SEAFOOD SAUCE
125 ml cream
15-30 ml tomato sauce
pinch cayenne pepper or paprika
dash of brandy (optional)

SPICY YOGHURT DRESSING
250 ml plain yoghurt
5 ml lemon juice
5 ml curry powder

HORSERADISH SAUCE
125 ml creamed horseradish
60 ml cream

TAPENADE MAYONNAISE
200 g calamata olives, stoned and puréed
6-8 anchovy fillets, drained and finely chopped
2 cloves garlic, crushed
30 ml capers
2 large spring onions, finely chopped
80 ml olive oil

PESTO MAYONNAISE

Perfect for fish and chicken. It may be chilled for up to 5 days.

50 g (80 ml) salted peanuts
1-2 cloves garlic
125 ml tightly packed basil leaves
250 ml Mayonnaise (this page)

Whiz peanuts, garlic and basil in a food processor until it forms a fine paste. Whiz in mayonnaise, scoop into a bowl and chill until serving time.

Makes about 350 ml

HERBED TOMATO SAUCE

Use any of your favourite herbs in this sauce – basil is my best, but thyme, marjoram and origanum are also superb. Or mix and match the herbs if the fancy takes you. If substituting dried herbs, check for freshness and go easy on the quantity.

4 large, ripe tomatoes
  or 400 g tin tomatoes
2 onions, very finely chopped
30 ml olive or sunflower oil
2 ml crushed garlic
15 ml chopped herbs
  or 2 ml dried herbs
30 ml chopped parsley
  or 10 ml dried parsley
pinch sugar
pinch paprika
salt and milled black pepper

Skin and chop tomatoes. Sauté onion in oil until lightly browned. Add remaining ingredients and cook briskly, uncovered and stirring occasionally for 5-6 minutes till sauce thickens slightly. Check seasoning and adjust if necessary.

Purée the sauce or leave it chunky if preferred and serve hot or cool.

Serves 4

VARIATIONS
Finely sliced fresh chillies add a touch of heat, and stoned black olives make an interesting flavour and texture variation.

MAKE AHEAD
You may keep this sauce in the fridge for up to 4 days. It also freezes beautifully.

FRESH TOMATO AND CORIANDER SALSA

A passion for things Mexican brings us this zestful no-cook sauce.

2-3 large, ripe tomatoes, finely chopped
1 small onion, finely chopped
1-2 cloves garlic, crushed
2-3 red chillies, seeded and very finely chopped
30 ml olive oil
15 ml wine vinegar
5 ml sugar
2 ml salt
small bunch fresh coriander, roughly chopped

Toss ingredients together (except coriander), and set aside for at least 2 hours for the flavours to mingle, then chill. Stir in coriander just before serving.

Serves 4-6

68 SAUCES AND DRESSINGS

OLD MAN SAUCE

A steakhouse favourite from the sixties, great for any type of steak.

1 small onion, very finely chopped
2 ml crushed garlic
30 g (30 ml) butter
20 ml flour
20 ml Dijon mustard
5 ml English mustard
125 ml beef stock
200 ml cream
30 ml brandy
salt and milled black pepper

In a small saucepan soften onion and garlic in butter. Remove from the heat and blend in flour, mustards, stock and cream. Cook, stirring for a couple of minutes, then add brandy and season to taste with salt and pepper.
Serves 6-8

GREEN PEPPERCORN SAUCE

A classic steak sauce which does wonders for chicken as well. Simply change the stock to suit the dish.

1 small onion, very finely chopped
30 g (30 ml) butter
15 ml green peppercorns
30 ml brandy (optional)
15 ml flour
250 ml beef or chicken stock
5 ml Dijon or French mustard
125 ml cream
salt and milled black pepper

In a small saucepan soften onion in butter. Add peppercorns, mashing some; leaving some whole for appearance sake. Remove the pot from the heat, add warmed brandy and flame. Blend in flour, then add stock, mustard and cream. Boil, stirring constantly at first, until the sauce reduces and thickens. This will take about 3 minutes.
  Check seasoning: if you've used homemade stock you may wish to add a touch of salt and a little black pepper.
Serves 6-8

QUICK SATAY SAUCE

Variations of this Indonesian sauce are concocted around the world, varying from place to place in components and fire. Here the traditional ingredients of peanuts, coconut and chilli are balanced in an exotic, spicy mix. It keeps well for up to a week.

200 ml coconut milk *
15 ml cornflour
60 ml peanut butter (smooth or crunchy)
30 ml soy sauce
30 ml medium sherry
5 ml sesame oil
5 ml crushed green ginger
  or 2 ml ground ginger
1 ml ground cumin
1 ml chilli powder
salt

* Available tinned or powdered. Alternatively blend 200 ml desiccated coconut in 300 ml hot water in a food processor or blender, then strain.

Combine ingredients in a small saucepan, bring to the boil and simmer, stirring, until smooth and thickened. Transfer to a suitable serving bowl and serve warm or cool.
Serves 6-8

BARBECUE SAUCE

A traditional Yankee sauce for those with a passion for heat.

1 large onion, finely chopped
2 large cloves garlic, crushed
30 ml sunflower oil
10 ml crushed green ginger
  or 5 ml ground ginger
125 ml tomato purée
125 ml wine vinegar
80 ml Worcestershire sauce
60 ml brown sugar
5 ml dry English mustard
2 ml chilli powder
5 ml paprika
15 ml lemon juice
2 bay leaves
5 ml salt
milled black pepper

In a medium saucepan soften onion and garlic in oil. Add remaining ingredients, cover and simmer for 5 minutes. Uncover and cook for a further 5 minutes or so until the sauce thickens. Stir occasionally, because as the sauce thickens there's a good chance of it burning.
  Remove bay leaves, pour sauce into a jar and refrigerate. It keeps well for a couple of months.
Makes about 450 ml

SAUCES AND DRESSINGS

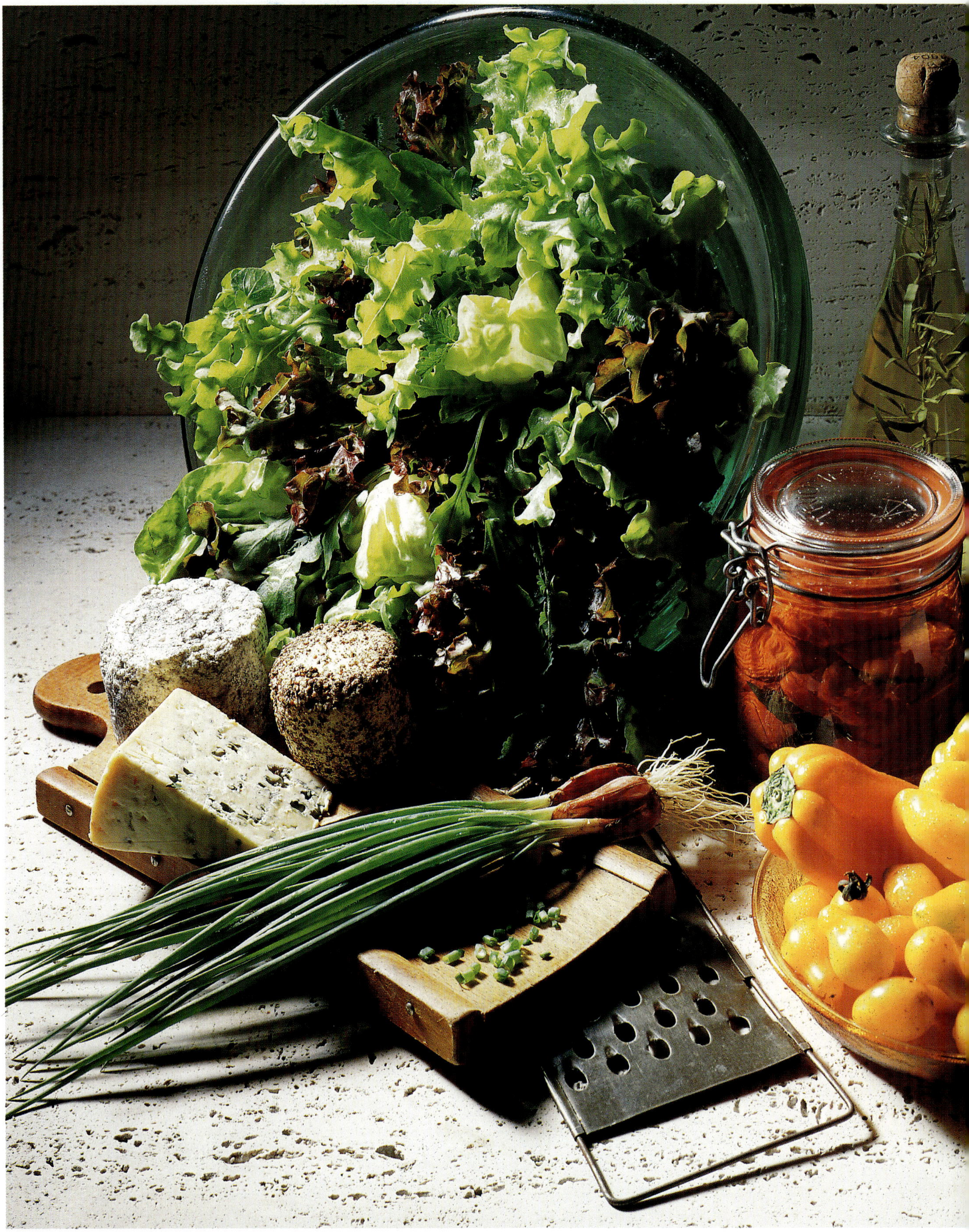

CHAPTER 8

SIDE DISHES

Freedom from cooking the main course in the kitchen allows more time to be innovative in other directions which are often much more fun.

Offer as many or as few side dishes as you wish. This is the one occasion where all restrictions should be cast aside. But please use the very best ingredients. The greatest joy, to my mind, is to be undecided until reaching the farm stall, then go to town, choosing the crispest, freshest fruit and vegetables to weave into amazing salads and other side dishes.

If your salad goodies are limp and lacking lustre, rustle up something which doesn't call for fresh vegetables. You'll find many ideas in the pages that follow. Some are simple, others are a touch more elaborate and are designed for posher occasions.

HERBED ORANGE, ONION AND OLIVE SALAD

For maximum flavour use gently-flavoured purple onions or substitute shallots or spring onions. And your vinegar and oil with care – rough stuff has a harsh flavour.

6 juicy oranges
45 ml vinegar (wine, cider or herbed)
80 ml olive oil or half olive, half sunflower oil
6-8 sage leaves, chopped
2 sprigs origanum, chopped
1 purple onion, sliced
milled black pepper
125 ml black olives

The Great Green Salad (page 72)

Peel oranges, cut in half and slice. Toss with vinegar, oil and herbs. Refrigerate for about 30 minutes then stir in onion and season with ground pepper. Dot olives on top and garnish with herbs.

Serve soon or the oranges will taste like onion and the simple charm of the thing will be completely lost.
Serves 6-8

KACHOOMER

An aromatic, flavourful Indian salad. If raw onion offends you, blanch it very briefly in boiling water before mixing with the tomato and the dressing.

6 firm, ripe tomatoes, cut into chunks
2 onions, fairly thickly sliced
lots of fresh coriander leaves

KACHOOMER DRESSING
15 ml cumin seeds
5 ml salt
10 ml sugar
125 ml wine vinegar
45 ml lemon juice

DRESSING Grind cumin seeds in a pestle and mortar, tip into a screw-topped jar, add remaining ingredients for the dressing and shake to mix.

Combine tomatoes and onions in a salad bowl, toss with the dressing. Scatter over plenty of coriander leaves just before serving.
Serves 6

MAKE AHEAD
Assemble this salad just before serving to retain the freshness of flavour. The dressing may be mixed a couple of days ahead and stored in the fridge. Give it a quick shake-up before dressing the salad and garnishing with coriander.

GREEK SALAD

A traditional Greek salad isn't just a basic green number with a perfunctory dotting of tomato, feta cheese and olives. It's a gutsy lettuce-less offering of these ingredients with onion and a herby, garlicky vinaigrette. Cucumber is an optional extra.

4 large, firm, ripe tomatoes, quartered
¼ English cucumber, sliced (optional)
1 small onion, finely sliced
100-150 g feta cheese, cubed
18-24 calamata olives
Herb Vinaigrette (page 67)
chopped parsley

Mix together tomato, cucumber and onion in a large bowl. Top with feta cubes and olives, dress liberally with vinaigrette and garnish with plenty of chopped parsley.
Serves 4

MAKE AHEAD
You may, but not too far ahead as tomato tends to get mushy. Cover and chill for no longer than 4 hours. Dress and garnish the salad just before serving.

CAESAR SALAD

This famous salad originated in Southern California in the 1920s. It's traditionally made with cos lettuce, but any type may be substituted.

2 cos lettuces or mixed salad greens

DRESSING
80 ml olive oil
45 ml lemon juice
1 clove garlic, crushed
3 anchovy fillets, drained and chopped
1 egg
milled black pepper

CROÛTONS
4 slices stale bread, de-crusted and cubed
1 clove garlic, chopped
olive or sunflower oil (or mix them)

GARNISH
45 ml grated Parmesan cheese
3 anchovy fillets, drained and sliced

CROÛTONS Heat oil in a frying pan, add garlic, allow it to turn golden, then toss in the cubed bread. Fry evenly on all sides, drain well on kitchen paper and cool. (Croûtons may be prepared several days ahead and stored in a cool spot in an airtight container.)

Assemble the salad just before serving. Tear lettuce leaves and toss into a bowl, blend dressing ingredients together and drizzle over the leaves. Sprinkle with cheese and garnish with anchovies and croûtons.
Serves 6

MARINATED CABBAGE AND CELERY

This is always a big hit at braai-time and keeps perfectly for up to 2 weeks in the fridge. Keep sealed and drain before transferring to a serving bowl.

½ cabbage
1 bunch soup celery
2 large onions
chopped parsley for garnish

DRESSING
250 ml sunflower oil
250 ml white vinegar
250 ml sugar
5 ml caraway seeds (optional)
salt and milled black pepper
1 ml dry English mustard

Shred cabbage very finely. Remove and discard celery leaves and chop ribs finely. Finely chop or slice onion. Mix vegetables together in a bowl.

Combine dressing ingredients in a saucepan and bring to the boil, stirring to dissolve the sugar. Pour hot dressing over the salad and toss to mix. Cover and chill before serving. A scattering of chopped parsley just before serving adds a nice touch of colour.
Serves 8-10

THE GREAT GREEN SALAD

Salads are no longer insipid appendages to a meaty main dish. They have stepped out of the wings to take their rightful place at centre stage.

Remember when the selection consisted of a miserable chopped tomato-onion-lettuce number and soggy coleslaw lethally laced with gluggy pink mayonnaise? No more. New-look salads fit the health and flavour dictates of today's more discerning diner with much emphasis on eye appeal.

Nor need a green salad be plain green – it's more often a melange of mixed leaves of varied hue studded with fresh herbs and crisp vegetables, raw or blanched as whim dictates.

Choose from cocktail tomatoes, infant carrots, baby broccoli and cauliflower florets, the slimmest green beans, sliced mushrooms, snow peas, asparagus tips and chubby little potatoes boiled in their jackets.

Some member of the onion family is obligatory – choose snipped chives, slim spring onions, sliced shallots or finely slivered leeks or onions.

If your life just isn't complete without some serious protein, turn the thing into a more substantial dish with nuts or slivers of cheese. Sliced hard-boiled eggs, crisp bacon and croûtons add a further dimension of texture.

And don't forget that floods of ubiquitous (and always over-flavoured) bottled dressings have moved over for a discreet gloss of extra-virgin olive oil and a dash of balsamic vinegar or a squeeze of lemon juice, and the merest suggestion of salt and pepper.

Lovers of vinaigrette are welcome to dress their salad accordingly. See page 67 for the recipes.

COLESLAW

The quintessential portable salad. If necessary prepare it a day ahead and give it a toss before serving.

¼ cabbage, very finely shredded
1 red or green pepper, seeded and sliced
1-2 ribs celery, chopped
3-4 carrots, coarsely grated
2 fat leeks or 1 medium onion, finely sliced
60 ml sultanas (optional)
60 ml chopped parsley
   (don't substitute dried parsley)

DRESSING
200 ml Mayonnaise (page 68)
125 ml plain yoghurt
salt and milled black pepper
squeeze of lemon juice

GARNISH
extra chopped parsley

Mix all the vegetables together with sultanas and parsley. Mix together and pour over dressing and toss well, then tip it into a serving dish, cover and chill until serving time.
   Garnish with freshly chopped parsley just before serving.
Serves 8-10

NUT AND FETA SLAW WITH ANCHOVY DRESSING

Not an ordinary slaw by any stretch of the imagination. This one has plenty of flavour twists to liven things up.

¼ cabbage, finely shredded
1 red or yellow pepper, seeded and finely sliced
1 Granny Smith apple, cored and cut into small chips
2 leeks, finely sliced
100 g salted peanuts
100 g feta cheese
plenty of chopped parsley
   (don't use dried parsley)

ANCHOVY VINAIGRETTE
125 ml olive or sunflower oil
30 ml wine or cider vinegar
30 ml dry sherry
8 anchovy fillets, chopped
milled black pepper
pinch of sugar
dash of dry English mustard

In a large bowl toss together cabbage, pepper, apple and leek. Blend dressing ingredients together, pour over, toss well, cover and refrigerate for a couple of hours to allow the flavours to mingle.
   Just before serving, tip the salad into a serving dish and top with nuts, crumbled feta and chopped parsley.
Serves 8-10

APPLE, CELERY AND PECAN SALAD

An all-time favourite that tastes divine and packs a powerful crunch.

2-3 Granny Smith apples
4 ribs celery, washed and trimmed
2 small leeks, very finely sliced,
   (green parts too)
100 g pecan nuts, crumbled
60 ml chopped parsley
   (don't use dried parsley)

DRESSING
200 ml Mayonnaise (page 68)
125 ml plain yoghurt
salt and milled black pepper
squeeze of lemon juice

Core the apples – peel first if you prefer – then slice. String and chop the celery (use some of the leaves, too, finely chopped). Mix with leeks, nuts and parsley. Mix ingredients for dressing, pour over salad, toss gently and refrigerate until required. Nasturtium flowers and leaves make a distinctive garnish.
Serves 4-6

MAKE AHEAD
If the salad has to hang about for any length of time, add the nuts at the last moment so they don't lose their crunch. Give it all a final mix just before serving.

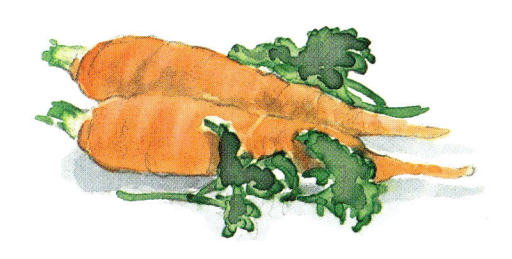

ORIENTAL NOODLE AND NUT SALAD

This marinated medley of noodles, nuts and vegetables, includes wonderful flavour and texture variations.

200 g medium-shape noodles
   (any design you fancy)
2 carrots, sliced into matchstick-sized bits
2 fat spring onions, finely sliced
1 red or green pepper, seeded and diced
2-3 spinach leaves
60 ml salted peanuts

DRESSING
80 ml sunflower oil
80 ml wine vinegar
15 ml soy sauce
5 ml brown sugar
5 ml sesame oil (optional)
2 ml prepared English mustard
2 ml crushed green ginger
   or ¼ ml dried ginger
salt and milled black pepper

Cook noodles in plenty of salted boiling water (don't let them get too soft), drain well and toss with carrots, spring onion and green or red pepper.
   Blend ingredients for dressing, mix into salad, cover and refrigerate for several hours, tossing occasionally. Just before serving, shred spinach finely and add it to the salad with the peanuts. Tip salad into a pretty serving bowl.
Serves 8

VARIATIONS
☐ If you prefer a thicker dressing add a spoonful of mayonnaise.
☐ Mix a 400 g tin of whole kernel corn, well drained, into the salad in place of the nuts.

SIDE DISHES

BACON BANANAS

Peel and lightly salt firm, skinned bananas, then wrap with rindless streaky bacon, working diagonally from one end to the other. Secure bacon with toothpicks and braai over hot coals just until the bacon forms a crisp and crunchy jacket.

If you wish to prepare these ahead of time, brush bananas with lemon juice before wrapping in bacon. Chill for up to 4 hours before braaiing.

STIR-FRIED SPINACH WITH BACON, TOMATOES AND FETA

A great looking, quick and easy dish. You could even whip it up in a frying pan over the coals.

- 1 large bunch spinach, washed and drained
- 4-6 rashers rindless, streaky bacon
- sunflower oil for cooking
- 12 cocktail tomatoes
- 100 g feta cheese, cut into blocks
- salt and milled black pepper
- 30 ml balsamic vinegar

Cut off and discard the thickest parts of the spinach stems and slice fairly thickly.

Slice bacon into smallish bits and fry crisply in a little oil in a wide saucepan. Add tomatoes and fry for about 30 seconds. Mix in spinach, cover and steam gently for a few minutes – it shouldn't be too limp. Season with salt, pepper and vinegar, add feta cheese, heat through and serve immediately.

Serves 4

FIGS IN BACON

During the short fig season these are a permanent part of our braai repertoire – they are positively addictive. And they don't object to being prepared a day ahead of time. Refrigerate in a closed container until braai-time.

Choose figs that are ripe but firm. Peel and salt lightly, then wrap in rindless streaky bacon, securing floppy ends with toothpicks. Braai over hot coals until bacon is as crisp as can be and figs are hot and tender. Keep warm on the edges of the grid until serving time.

HOT SPINACH SALAD WITH BACON AND MUSHROOMS

An unusual and tangy mix of ingredients. Fry croûtons and bacon ahead of time if you wish, and prepare the rest of the salad at the last minute.

- 1 bunch fresh, young spinach, washed and drained
- 4 slices white bread, decrusted and cubed
- sunflower oil for cooking
- 125 g rindless, streaky bacon, finely chopped
- 30 ml Worcestershire sauce
- juice of 1 lemon
- 150 g button mushrooms, sliced
- milled black pepper

Cut off and discard the thickest parts of the spinach stems, chop leaves roughly and set aside. In a wide frying pan crisply fry bread cubes in oil. Drain on kitchen paper and set aside. Fry bacon bits until crispy in the same pan, drain and set aside to cool.

Add Worcestershire sauce and lemon juice to the remaining fat in the frying pan, toss in spinach and mushrooms, stir it all up then cover and steam until vegetables are limp but not overcooked.

Pile salad onto a serving platter, top with croûtons and bacon bits and season with a little milled pepper. Serve at once.

Serves 6

BRAAIED BANANAS

These are particularly pleasing with chicken and pork. Place firm bananas, skins and all, on the grid. Braai over medium coals for 20-30 minutes until cooked through. It's impossible to tell when a banana is done until it's skinned. It's also impossible to overcook them, so leave them round the edges of the grid for as long as you wish before serving.

For crisper results slice unpeeled bananas lengthwise, brush the cut edges with melted butter, squeeze on a little lemon juice and sprinkle lightly with brown sugar. Braai the cut side first until lightly browned, then turn for the final 10 minutes' cooking time. Scoop the tender flesh from the skins and serve warm.

CHARRED VEGETABLES

Very Mediterranean, these colourful vegetables are quick to cook in the oven or over the coals. Mix and match your favourites, this list is only a suggestion.

- 1 onion, quartered or 8 shallots or large spring onions, trimmed
- 2 smallish brinjals, quartered lengthwise
- 4 baby marrows, halved
- 1 red and 1 yellow pepper, seeded and cut into big flat pieces
- 4 brown mushrooms
- thickly sliced mealies
- olive oil
- sea salt and milled black pepper

Toss the prepared vegetables liberally in olive oil – if you're grilling them in the oven do this in the grill pan; use a deep bowl if they are to be braaied. Arrange in a single layer in the grill pan, or in a hinged grid for the braai and season with salt and pepper. Grill slowly at first to soften vegetables, then fiercely to char the edges. Total cooking time is no longer than 10-15 minutes.

Tip vegetables into a hot serving dish, season with extra salt, pepper and olive oil if you wish. Rough bread makes a perfect accompaniment.

Serves 4

Stir-Fried Spinach with Bacon, Tomatoes and Feta (page 74)

SIDE DISHES 75

VEGETABLE KEBABS

These super skewers-full are the centre of attraction at a non-meat braai. Choose vegetables which will stand up to a certain amount of manhandling on the skewer. Those which require longer cooking may be par-cooked before assembling. And remember to aim for a satisfying flavour and colour combination.

CHOOSE FROM
**pickling onions
cocktail tomatoes
Brussels sprouts
chunks of red, green or yellow peppers
button mushrooms
thickly sliced baby marrows
sliced mealie wheels
fresh or tinned pineapple chunks
cauliflower and broccoli florets
tinned artichoke hearts
chunks of brinjal**

FLAVOURING
**olive oil or Garlic Butter (page 22)
salt and milled black pepper**

Take your pick and stab the vegetables onto bamboo skewers which are slim enough to pierce the vegetables without breaking them.

A basting sauce is vital to keep kebabs moist. Garlic butter is best, though a gloss of olive oil or melted butter and a seasoning with salt and pepper will do the trick. Baste frequently while braaiing the kebabs over medium coals. Avoid turning too frequently which will increase the risk of their falling apart.

MAKE AHEAD
Assemble, cover and refrigerate the kebabs for up to 24 hours ahead of time.

FOIL-BAKED VEGETABLES
Onions
Onions in foil enhance anything and everything, from steak to seafood. Choose medium specimens, 1-2 per person, depending on whether you're serving other side dishes as well. Slice a sliver off each end, but leave the skin on. Cutting off the ends allows you to detect unsavoury brown centres (reject these onions forthwith) and allows your guests to easily pop out the tender centres.

Wrap singly or in groups in a double layer of heavy foil, and bake nestled in medium coals for at least 30 minutes, or until the parcel becomes nicely squashy under pressure.

Remove from the coals and keep warm beside the fire until serving time.

Butternut
Choose smaller specimens (they're sweeter and a touch more tender), slice lengthways into quarters and discard the pips. Wrap in foil and bake in medium-cool coals for about 45 minutes. When they're done, the parcel feels tender when prodded.

Gem squash
Halve and de-pip squash and fill the cavity with a knob of butter and a dash of grated nutmeg. Wrap in foil and cook in medium-cool coals for about 30 minutes until tender. Serve with an extra dot of butter and a sprinkling of salt and pepper.

SWEETCORN FRITTERS

I hear screeches of horror whenever I dust off this recipe. But in a camp-fire setting there's really nothing nicer.

**400 g tin creamed sweetcorn
2 eggs
125 ml cake or all-purpose flour
2 ml baking powder
1 ml salt
1/4 ml cayenne pepper (optional)
milled black pepper**

Mix together sweetcorn and eggs, sift in dry ingredients and mix well. Fry tablespoonfuls in hot oil until crispy brown on both sides. Take care: if insufficiently cooked they're all yukky in the middle.

Drain very well on several layers of kitchen paper laid atop a wad of newspaper, then arrange on a warmed serving plate. Continue cooking the fritters until all the batter has been used up.
Makes about 24

BRAAIED MEALIES
Also known as corn, sweetcorn, maize and Indian corn, mealies are most often boiled and buttered. But they're equally delicious cooked gently over the coals.

The downside is that it's not a dish which can be enjoyed to the full in polite society, as anyone who's listened, fascinated, to a mealie-muncher will agree, so choose your munching mates with care.

Mealies must be fresh – straight from the plant to the fire if this is at all possible. Buy them husks and all, for the silk is a pretty good indicator of freshness. Kernels should be plump and juicy-looking.

Fold back the husk, remove and discard the silk, then replace the husks. Soak mealies in cold water for 30 minutes, then braai for 20-30 minutes, or up to 45 minutes if you prefer well browned, smoky kernels. Turn frequently to ensure even cooking and watch for over-cooking which toughens the mealies.

If you can only buy mealies which have been stripped of their outer layers don't despair. After soaking, wrap them in foil which will take the place of the husks.

Mealies may also be braaied without the soaking or wrapping procedure. Cut into chunks (for quicker cooking and easier eating) and braai over medium coals until tender. Pre-cooking for a short while will reduce the cooking time and ensure more tender kernels.

SIDE DISHES

BRAAIED MUSHROOMS

Here's one instance where biggest is best – at least as far as flavour goes. Baby button mushrooms are attractive skewered and grilled but the succulence and flavour of big daddy mushrooms gives them the edge in the braai stakes. Another plus is that they require scant attention on the grid.

Even though they shrink while they cook, mushrooms are filling, so one may safely allow slightly less meat when serving a generous portion of mushrooms at the same time.

Cultivated mushrooms need only be wiped with a damp cloth then placed on the grid. Braai just long enough to cook them through without rendering them mushy and meaningless – 5-15 minutes depending on size and coal heat. Just add salt, milled pepper and a squeeze of lemon juice. If there's no lemon tree handy, a splosh of wine or beer will do almost as well. Brush mushrooms with oil, melted butter or Garlic Butter (page 22) and turn occasionally as they cook.

VARIATION: **MARINATED MUSHROOMS**
Add extra flavour by marinating your mushrooms before braaiing – up to one hour is all they require. This mixture will be sufficient for about 500 g mushrooms.

MARINADE
60 ml sunflower oil
125 ml dry white wine
juice of ½ lemon
15 ml chopped marjoram
   or 2 ml dried marjoram
30 ml chopped parsley
   or 5 ml dried parsley
2 ml fennel seeds

Mix all ingredients together and pour over mushrooms. Cover and set aside until required.

MOZZARELLA MUSHROOMS WITH HERBED TOMATO

A tasty side dish that also makes an excellent starter.

6 large black mushrooms
salt and milled black pepper
lemon juice
Herbed Tomato Sauce
   (page 68)
12 thin slices mozzarella cheese

Prepare the tomato sauce, cooking away enough of the moisture to make it nice and thick. Preheat oven to 200 °C.

Wipe mushrooms clean with a damp cloth, remove stems, place side-by-side in an oven-to-table baking dish and season with salt, pepper and lemon juice.

Spoon tomato sauce into the hollows and top each with two slices of cheese. Bake for 8-10 minutes – just long enough to cook the mushrooms, heat the filling and sizzle the cheese.
Serves 4-6

MAKE AHEAD
The prepared but uncooked dish may be refrigerated for up to a day. Bake just before serving.

BANANA BEANS

Sounds like an unlikely combination, but it's a very successful one, and especially popular with younger members of the family. Please don't assemble the dish longer than 4 hours before serving as it doesn't do the bananas any good at all.

4-6 bananas
400 g tin baked beans in
   tomato sauce
125 ml Mayonnaise (page 68)

Skin and slice bananas and mix lightly with beans and mayonnaise. Serve cold – and not too long after preparation, as the banana tends to become mushy the longer it has to wait.
Serves 6

MUSHROOMS FILLED WITH SPICY RICE

A good choice for when the party includes non meat-eaters, although those with carnivorous inclinations will certainly be equally impressed.

6 large black mushrooms, wiped

SPICY RICE STUFFING
200 ml chopped spring onion
50 g (50 ml) butter
5 ml turmeric
125 ml uncooked rice
375 ml chicken stock
5 ml chopped thyme
   or 1 ml dried thyme
milled black pepper
30 ml chopped parsley
   or 5 ml dried parsley
12 calamata olives, stoned
   and finely chopped

TOPPING
grated Parmesan cheese

Cut out the stems and chop finely. Place mushrooms in a baking dish.
STUFFING In a medium saucepan, soften spring onion in some of the butter. Stir in chopped mushroom stems, turmeric and rice, then add stock, thyme and pepper. (Add salt only if non-salted stock has been used.) Cover and simmer very gently for 20-25 minutes until the rice is done and all the stock has been absorbed. Remove from the heat and stir in parsley, olives and remaining butter.

Preheat oven to 200 °C. Fill mushrooms with rice, dust with Parmesan and bake uncovered for 10-15 minutes.
Serves 4-6

VARIATION
Brinjals are just as delicious as mushrooms in this recipe. Halve them, scoop out and chop some of the flesh, and add this to the rice instead of the chopped mushroom stems.

MAKE AHEAD
The filled mushrooms may be refrigerated for up to a day. Add the cheese and bake just before serving.

SIDE DISHES

BIG BEAN MIX

A hot and hearty dish. Other tinned beans may be substituted, but the three specified give a great flavour and colour contrast. If you have some bacon handy, chop it and fry with the onion. Chips of apple make a nice variation too.

1 large onion, roughly chopped
4 rashers rindless streaky bacon, chopped
sunflower oil for cooking
400 g tin red kidney beans, drained
400 g tin white kidney beans, drained
400 g tin baked beans in tomato sauce
400 g tin tomatoes, chopped
salt and milled black pepper
cayenne pepper

Fry onion and bacon in oil until all the fat has rendered and the onion is golden brown. Add remaining ingredients, season to taste and heat through.
Serves 8-10

VARIATION
Hot things up by using chilli beans instead of red kidney beans and add a crunchy topping: mix 100 g crushed corn chips with 125 ml grated Cheddar cheese and pile on top. Bake in a hot oven for 15-20 minutes.

LENTILS AND BEANS WITH HERB VINAIGRETTE

Beans and lentils join forces to make a meagre amount of meat go further. Other tinned beans may be substituted, but for the best colour and flavour, lima and red kidney beans are impossible to beat.

100 g dried brown lentils
400 g tin lima beans, drained
400 g tin red kidney beans, drained
3-4 ribs celery, sliced
1 smallish onion, very finely chopped
Herb Vinaigrette (page 67)

GARNISH
mint sprigs

Place lentils in a small pot with cold water to cover, bring to the boil and cook for 5 minutes. Set aside and soak for an hour. Drain, refresh under cold running water and salt lightly.

Combine lentils, beans, celery and onion, pour over the dressing and toss lightly. Leave the salad to marinate at room temperature for an hour or two or refrigerate overnight.

Just before serving, toss the salad and garnish with fresh mint sprigs.
Serves 8-10

YANKEE BAKED BEANS

The genuine tin-plate variety, equally delicious hot or coolish.

250 g dried sugar beans or white kidney beans
3 onions, chopped
5 ml crushed garlic
3 whole cloves
1 bay leaf
5 ml salt
250 g rindless bacon, chopped
100 g brown sugar
125 ml dark vinegar
5 ml prepared English mustard

Soak washed beans overnight in plenty of cold water. Drain, rinse and tip into a pot. Cover with more cold water and add half of the chopped onion, garlic, cloves, bay leaf and salt. Cover and simmer for 1 hour.

Preheat oven to 160 °C. Into the beans mix bacon and remaining onion, sugar, vinegar and mustard. Transfer the mixture to an ovenproof baking dish. Bake uncovered for about 1½ hours until beans are tender and caramelised, stirring every 30 minutes. Keep an eye on them towards the end of the cooking time – the beans have a nasty habit of burning the moment you turn your back.
Serves 6-8

MAKE AHEAD
Store covered and refrigerated for up to 4 days. Reheat as and when required.

SOUSBOONTJIES

A great South African favourite and easy to do yourself.

500 g dried white kidney beans
50 g (50 ml) butter
60 ml white sugar
125 ml white vinegar
5 ml salt
2 ml white pepper

Wash beans and soak overnight in plenty of cold water. Drain, add fresh water – just enough to cover the beans – cover and simmer very slowly for about an hour until tender. The cooking time depends entirely on the age of the beans.

Stir in remaining ingredients and simmer uncovered until the sauce thickens slightly and the beans are soft but still whole. This should take approximately 30 minutes. Stir occasionally. When judging done-ness bear in mind that the sauce thickens as it cools.

Spoon hot sousboontjies into hot sterilised jars, seal and store in a dark, cool cupboard. Once opened, refrigerate.
About 2,5 litres

COAL-ROASTED GARLIC

The longer it cooks, the milder the garlic flavour. It's a pungent accompaniment for meat or baked potatoes.

plump whole heads of garlic
olive oil

Break open the garlic heads just sufficiently to separate the cloves a little. Leave on the white papery covering. Drizzle liberally with olive oil and wrap in a double layer of heavy foil, shiny side in. Roast for 1½ hours in an oven preheated to 200 °C or nestle in coolish coals (push a scoop to one side especially). Cooking time in the fire will be less – about 1 hour.

To serve, unwrap the garlic and offer as is. The cloves may simply be split open and the garlic smeared onto the meat.

BRINJAL AND ONION PICKLE

A super spicy side dish that may be served hot or cool with red meat. It may be prepared up to 3 days ahead. Serve at room temperature for maximum flavour.

2-3 brinjals (about 400 g in total)
salt and milled black pepper
sunflower oil for cooking
2 onions, finely sliced
1 green chilli, seeded and finely sliced
5 ml crushed garlic
  or 2 ml garlic flakes
5 ml crushed green ginger
  or 1 ml dried ginger
5 ml brown sugar
15 ml oyster sauce (optional)
2 large tomatoes, skinned and roughly chopped

Slice brinjals (leave skin on), sprinkle with salt and pile into a colander. Set aside for about 30 minutes. This extracts all the bitter juices. Rinse well and pat dry with kitchen paper.

In a saucepan with a well-fitting lid fry brinjal briefly in hot oil, a few slices at a time, just until lightly coloured on both sides. Drain well on kitchen paper. Add a little more oil to the pan as necessary. Toss onion into the pan and fry until golden brown. Add garlic, ginger, sugar, oyster sauce and tomatoes with a little salt and ground black pepper. Cover and simmer very gently for 5 minutes.

Mix in brinjal, cover and simmer for 5 minutes more. Check seasoning, tip into a serving bowl and serve hot or cool.
Serves 6-8

Brinjal and Onion Pickle

Cover with foil and bake for 45 minutes. Uncover, top brinjals with cheese, increase heat to 220 °C and bake for 10 minutes more until cheese sizzles and browns.
Serves 4-6

MAKE AHEAD
The prepared, unbaked brinjals may be covered and refrigerated for up to a day.

CRUMBED CAULIFLOWER AND TOMATOES

A fairly substantial vegetable dish, great for a winter braai.

1 cauliflower, cut into florets
12 cocktail tomatoes
 or 2 large, ripe tomatoes, sliced
salt and milled black pepper
50 g (50 ml) butter
250 ml soft breadcrumbs
125 ml chopped fresh herbs (mostly parsley, but mix in thyme and origanum)

Preheat oven to 200 °C. Cook cauliflower florets in boiling, salted water until crisp-tender, drain well, then arrange in a casserole. Tuck tomatoes or tomato slices here and there. Season with a light sprinkling of salt and pepper.

Melt butter and stir in the herbs and crumbs and scatter over the cauliflower. Bake for 10-20 minutes until the vegetables are piping hot and the crumbs are nice and crisp.
Serves 6-8

MAKE AHEAD
Assemble the dish prior to baking, cover and refrigerate for up to a day ahead. Serve fresh from the oven.

VARIATIONS
☐ Mix together broccoli and cauliflower for a more colourful dish.
☐ Fry 4-6 chopped bacon rashers in the butter before frying the crumbs.
☐ A scattering of caraway seeds adds a different dimension, too.

Slaphakskeentjies (page 81)

NIÇOISE BRINJALS

These are filled with the distinctive, lusty flavours of the sunny Mediterranean. Bear in mind that brinjals must be firm and glossy, with not a wrinkle in sight. If there are none available don't compromise - choose another side dish!

3 medium brinjals
salt and milled black pepper
60 ml olive or sunflower oil
2 large, ripe tomatoes
125 ml fresh breadcrumbs
60 ml sultanas
12 black olives, stoned and chopped
60 ml chopped parsley
 or 10 ml dried parsley
15 ml chopped basil leaves
 or 2 ml dried basil
2 ml crushed garlic
150 g mozzarella cheese, sliced

Slice brinjals lengthwise and scoop out some of the flesh to make a hollow. Chop this and reserve. Sprinkle salt into shells and over chopped brinjal and set aside for 30 minutes. Preheat oven to 180 °C. Pat brinjals dry, brush shells with half the oil and place in a baking dish.

Finely chop one tomato and mix with the chopped brinjal, crumbs, sultanas, olives, parsley, basil, garlic and remaining oil. Season with salt and ground pepper. Fill brinjal shells and top with remaining tomato, finely sliced.

SIDE DISHES

RATATOUILLE

Offer this marvellous vegetable melange unrivalled by lesser side dishes, except perhaps new potatoes or crusty bread. Aim for perfection of texture and colour – ratatouille is so easily overcooked to mushy anonymity. Season well but not indiscriminately; purists use just parsley and basil, but you may enjoy adding other freshly-plucked herbs as well. And for extra flavour, feel free to add a dash of tomato paste.

1-2 brinjals, cut in chunks (skin on)
45 ml olive oil
2 large onions, sliced
2 cloves garlic, crushed
2-3 baby marrows, thickly sliced
1 red and 1 green pepper, cut into big chunks
4 ripe tomatoes, skinned and chopped
  or 400 g tin tomatoes
30 ml chopped parsley
  or 10 ml dried parsley
15 ml chopped basil
  or 2 ml dried basil
1 bay leaf, sprig thyme, sprig marjoram (optional)
5 ml sugar
salt and milled black pepper

Sprinkle brinjals with salt and set aside for 30 minutes. Pat dry.

In a medium pot sauté onion and garlic in hot oil until tender and golden. Add remaining ingredients, cover and simmer for 15-20 minutes until vegetables are tender. Check seasoning. Serve piping hot or cool – it's delicious either way.
Serves 6-8

MAKE AHEAD
Ratatouille reheats perfectly after 3-4 days in the fridge. Just take care not to overcook it.

SLAPHAKSKEENTJIES

This traditional Cape onion salad is best served at room temperature.

1 kg pickling onions, skinned

SOUR EGG SAUCE
3 eggs
30 ml white sugar
5 ml dry English mustard
2 ml salt
125 ml white vinegar
30 ml water
200 ml milk or cream

Cook onions in salted boiling water until just tender but not overcooked. Drain and set aside. In a heavy saucepan whisk eggs, sugar, mustard and salt until creamy. Add vinegar, water and milk or cream and cook very gently over low heat until the sauce thickens. Pour hot sauce over the onions and serve as the dish cools down.
Serves 6-8

MAKE AHEAD
The sauce should be made just before serving. The onions, however, may be prepared several hours ahead.

CHEESY ONIONS

Cheese and onion flavours mingle marvellously. In this case, baby onions napped with a light cheese sauce.

500 g pickling onions, skinned
50 g (50 ml) butter
30 ml flour
125 ml milk
1 ml dry English mustard
60 ml sour cream
80 ml grated Cheddar cheese
salt and milled black pepper

Place onions in a pot with sufficient cold water to cover. Boil uncovered for 5-7 minutes or until tender.

Remove onions with a slotted spoon. Boil stock uncovered until reduced to about 150 ml. Strain and reserve to use in the sauce.

SAUCE Melt butter in a clean saucepan. Remove from the heat and blend in flour, stock, milk and mustard. Cook, stirring, until smooth and thickened. Season with salt and pepper. Add sour cream and cheese, stir until melted and check consistency – it shouldn't be thicker than cream or the dish will be gluggy.

Turn onions in the sauce, heat through and tip it all into a warmed serving dish.
Serves 6

MAKE AHEAD
These onions may be made a day ahead and reheated. In this case, cover and heat through in the oven, on the stove over very gentle heat or in the microwave.

GLAZED ONIONS WITH TOMATOES AND CORIANDER

An interesting spicy dish, easily prepared up to 3 days ahead and reheated when it's time to serve. But please don't use a lesser substitute for wine or cider vinegar – it'll ruin the flavour.

500 g pickling onions, skinned
80 g butter
5 ml whole coriander seeds
2 cloves garlic, finely chopped
125 ml wine or cider vinegar
2 ml salt
milled black pepper
250 g cocktail tomatoes

Heat butter in a small pot until sizzling, toss in onions and coriander and cook, turning occasionally, until lightly browned. Add garlic, vinegar, salt and pepper, cover and cook gently just until onions are tender. Add tomatoes and cook without the lid for a minute or two more. The sauce will thicken nicely.

Transfer vegetables to a serving dish and serve warm.
Serves 4-6

VARIATION
Zap things up with a touch of heat. Add a couple of fresh chillies, seeded and very finely sliced, or a dash of chilli powder.

SIDE DISHES 81

RICE SALAD

Always popular and convenient to make up to a day ahead. The ingredients are fairly flexible, but avoid those – like tomatoes and cucumber – which draw moisture and make the salad soggy.

125 ml uncooked rice
60 ml sultanas
2 ml salt
375 ml cold water
1 small onion, finely chopped
1 red or green pepper, finely chopped
1-2 carrots, grated
2-3 ribs celery, finely sliced
200 g cooked or tinned peas
400 g tin whole-kernel corn, drained
30 ml chopped parsley
   (don't substitute dried parsley)

DRESSING
125 ml Mayonnaise (page 68)
125 ml plain yoghurt
salt and milled black pepper
2 ml paprika (optional)

Combine rice, sultanas, salt and water in a large saucepan, cover and bring to the boil. Simmer until all the liquid has been absorbed and rice is cooked.

Tip into a large bowl and toss with remaining salad ingredients. Mix dressing ingredients, pour over salad and toss. Cover and chill.

Just before serving give the salad a final toss and garnish with extra chopped parsley if it's handy.
Serves 8-10

VARIATION
A touch of curry is lovely in the dressing; add about 15 ml.

DIRTY RICE

Cajun recipes from America's Deep South are zapped with flavour, and this spicy rice dish is a great example. The addition of mushrooms isn't traditional, but they add a nice texture variation.

30 g (30 ml) butter
375 ml uncooked rice
500 ml chicken stock
100 g button mushrooms, chopped
15 ml Worcestershire sauce
1 large, ripe tomato, finely chopped
1 ml dried origanum
½ ml ground chilli
2 ml salt
milled black pepper

In a deep pot lightly sizzle rice in butter. Stir in remaining ingredients, cover and simmer until all the liquid has been absorbed. Fluff up with a fork and tip into a warmed serving bowl.
Serves 6-8

TO GARNISH
Let your imagination run riot, but never serve your Dirty Rice unadorned. Stay in the appropriate mood with fresh coriander, sliced avocado, chilli flowers or even sliced chorizo sausage. If you're feeling particularly flamboyant, add the lot!

MAKE AHEAD
All rice dishes reheat perfectly. The microwave works best (use full power and stir after every 2-3 minutes until it's piping hot), or toss the rice about in a buttery frying pan.

BAKED POTATOES

No matter how fancy things get, baked spuds are all but compulsory at any self-respecting braai.

1-2 potatoes per person
olive or sunflower oil
sea salt or coarse salt

TO SERVE *choose from...*
pats of chilled butter
lashings of sour cream
blobs of cream cheese
   or cottage cheese
spoonfuls of caviare

TO GARNISH *choose from...*
snipped chives
crisply cooked, crumbled bacon
grated cheese
chopped red or green pepper
sliced mushrooms fried in butter
fried onion rings

Choose potatoes that are perfect, even-sized and blemish-free. Scrub under running water, rub with a little oil and season well with salt.
FOIL-BAKING Wrap individually or in groups in a double layer of heavy foil. Many's the spud that has been burnt to a cinder because of a mingy wrapper, so please don't skimp!

Nestle your potatoes in medium coals (scoop some to one side while your fire continues to burn in readiness for the meat). Cook for 40-60 minutes, depending on the size of the potatoes and the heat of the coals. Turn parcels occasionally to ensure even baking and browning.

When done, open the foil slightly and keep the potatoes hot on the side of the fire. This will keep them crisp while they leisurely await the moment of serving.
OVEN-BAKING Sheer force of numbers may persuade you that it's simpler to oven-bake the potatoes. Give them the salt and oil treatment and bake at 200 °C until tender when pierced with a skewer. (About 40-60 minutes, depending on size, though par-cooking in a microwave oven will shorten the time.)

Time potatoes to coincide with the rest of the braai as they dry up and shrivel miserably when kept warm.

SIDE DISHES

Rice Salad (page 82)

POTATO AND ONION PARCEL

A tasty variation on the potato theme.

4 potatoes, scrubbed and cubed
2 onions, cut into chunks
salt and milled black pepper
butter

Pile the potato and onion chunks into a large piece of heavy foil. Season well with salt and pepper and dot generously with butter. Seal the parcel and wrap the whole thing again in another piece of foil.

Cook on a thick bed of coolish coals. Listen to the sizzle – it should be nice and gentle. If the coals are too hot, the ingredients will burn. What you're after is light browning of the bottom layer while the rest steams through gently.

Tip it all into a warmed serving bowl and garnish with chopped parsley.
Serves 4

VARIATIONS
Add thickly sliced button mushrooms to the parcel. Chopped fresh herbs and crushed garlic give extra flavour too.

POTATO AND COTTAGE CHEESE BAKE

Fast, family-proof and just a little luxurious! Use savoury cottage cheese or cheese with chives if you like.

500 g (about 4) potatoes, skinned and cubed
250 ml cream
1 egg
250 g tub chunky cottage cheese
60 ml finely chopped spring onion
60 ml chopped parsley
small bunch chives, snipped
salt and milled pepper

TOPPING
125 ml fresh breadcrumbs
60 ml grated Cheddar or Parmesan cheese

Preheat oven to 160 °C. Cook potatoes in a little salted water until just (only just!) cooked; drain well. Overcook them and your bake will be mushy.

Beat together cream and egg and mix gently into potato with cottage cheese, onion, parsley and chives. Season to taste with salt and pepper. Tip the mixture into a buttered casserole and sprinkle crumbs and cheese on top. Bake for about 30 minutes until piping hot then brown the topping under the oven griller. Serve the moment it's deliciously crunchy.
Serves 4-5

MAKE AHEAD
After assembling the dish, cover and refrigerate for up to a day. Bake just before serving, adding an extra 5 minutes cooking time.

ORANGE-GLAZED SWEET POTATO

South Africans love a little sweetness with their meat. This recipe fits the bill perfectly and it can be prepared a day or two ahead. There's no real need to add the whisky, unless you like a little luxury to lift a down-home recipe.

750 g sweet potatoes, skinned and cubed
100 g butter
30 ml brown sugar or honey
few slices green ginger
    or ½ ml dried ginger
1 stick cinnamon
finely grated rind and juice of
    1 orange
30 ml whisky (optional)

Preheat oven to 180 °C. Toss sweet potato cubes into a buttered baking dish. Melt butter, mix in remaining ingredients and pour over the potato. Cover with foil and bake for 40-50 minutes until potato is tender.

Uncover, baste with buttery sauce and grill until potato tips are crunchy and golden brown.
Serves 4-6

GREAT POTATO SALAD

This fabulous salad is often abused by cooks devoid of imagination. There's nothing as dreary as mushy, over-cooked potatoes with no more to raise the spirits than a trickle of bottled mayonnaise.

8 potatoes, scrubbed
1 bunch spring onions, trimmed and
    finely chopped
60 ml chopped dill pickle
2-3 hard-boiled eggs, chopped
60 ml chopped parsley
    (don't use dried parsley)

DRESSING
200 ml Mayonnaise (page 68)
125 ml plain yoghurt
salt and milled black pepper
squeeze of lemon juice
50 g blue cheese, crumbled (optional)

Boil potatoes in their jackets until tender. Cool, skin, dice and toss with spring onion, dill pickle, hard-boiled egg and most of the parsley (keep a little of this for garnish).

Blend dressing and add to salad. Toss gently until well mixed, then tip into a clean serving bowl. Garnish with remaining parsley and chill before serving.
Serves 8

MAKE AHEAD
Potato salad is fine for up to a day in the fridge. Keep it longer than that and your guests will know!

SIDE DISHES

HOT POTATO SALAD

Great for a cool-weather braai when a mayonnaisey potato salad doesn't appeal.

4 large potatoes
sunflower oil for cooking
100 g rindless streaky bacon rashers, chopped
1 onion, finely chopped
80 ml wine vinegar
salt and milled black pepper
small bunch chives, snipped

GARNISH
coriander leaves
chopped chervil or parsley

Boil potatoes in their jackets until tender. Peel and dice them when they're cool enough to handle.

Heat a little oil in a frying pan and gently fry the bacon until all the fat has rendered and the bacon is cooked. Stir in onion and cook until tender. Add potato and vinegar and toss gently until the potato breaks up a bit and the dish is piping hot. Season with salt and pepper and stir in snipped chives.

Pile the salad into a warmed serving dish and garnish with herbs.
Serves 4

MAKE AHEAD
Make the dish a day ahead and reheat in a hot oven, or use the microwave oven, tossing gently every 2-3 minutes until piping hot.

HERBED POTATO FRY

A rustic dish, which can be made in a hurry.

3-4 large potatoes, peeled and cut into large chunks
1 large onion, skinned and thickly sliced
butter and sunflower oil for cooking
1-2 cloves garlic, crushed (optional)
salt and milled black pepper
60 ml chopped, fresh herbs (chives, parsley, tarragon, thyme)

Toss potato, onion and garlic into lots of sizzling butter and oil. Season with salt and pepper and shake the frying pan to prevent potato from sticking.

Fry quickly, turning to brown potato bits on all sides. When they're done mix in the chopped herbs and continue to cook just until the aroma fills the room. Whatever you do, don't overcook the herbs or they'll be dull and unappealing.

Tip potatoes into a warm serving dish and serve at once, adding a scattering of chopped parsley for a touch of colour.
Serves 4

VARIATION
Extra vegetables wouldn't go amiss in this dish. Try chopped green pepper, whole baby mushrooms or a handful of finely sliced cabbage.

SWEET AND SOUR ONIONS

Tangy and good to make ahead. The flavour improves with keeping.

24-30 pickling onions, washed but unskinned
3-4 cloves garlic, chopped
2 ml powdered chicken stock
60 ml brown sugar
60 ml dark vinegar
45 ml tomato sauce
10 ml soy sauce
15 ml cornflour
125 ml cold water

Place onions, garlic and stock in a saucepan with just enough cold water to cover. Bring to the boil and cook uncovered for 3 minutes. Drain onions with a slotted spoon (reserve stock) and refresh with cold water. They're now easily skinned and the stock has taken on a lovely colour.

Boil stock, uncovered, until reduced to 125 ml. Return onions to the pot and add sugar, vinegar, tomato sauce, soy sauce and cornflour mixed with the cold water. Boil, stirring gently, until the sauce is slightly thickened and clear and the onions are crisp-tender. This will take about 5 minutes. Transfer to a warm serving dish and serve hot.
Serves 6-8

GARLICKY POTATO AND ONION WITH ROSEMARY

A designer potato dish with loads of flavour and eye-appeal.

1 kg (4-5) potatoes, well scrubbed
2 large onions
10 fat cloves garlic, peeled
60 ml olive oil
salt and milled black pepper
20 sprig-tips fresh rosemary

Preheat oven to 200 °C. Cut potatoes into chunks and toss into a baking dish (there's no need to peel first). Peel and chop onions roughly and add to the potato with the garlic.

Add olive oil and stir until everything is well coated. Season with salt and pepper and tuck in sprigs of rosemary here and there, saving some for a garnish. Cover with lightly oiled foil and bake for 20 minutes until vegetables are fairly tender though nowhere near the mushy stage which will spoil things totally.

Uncover, remove rosemary (the sprigs will burn) and grill for a further 10-15 minutes, stirring occasionally, until potatoes and onions are browned. Tip it all into a clean serving dish and garnish with fresh rosemary.
Serves 6-8

SIDE DISHES

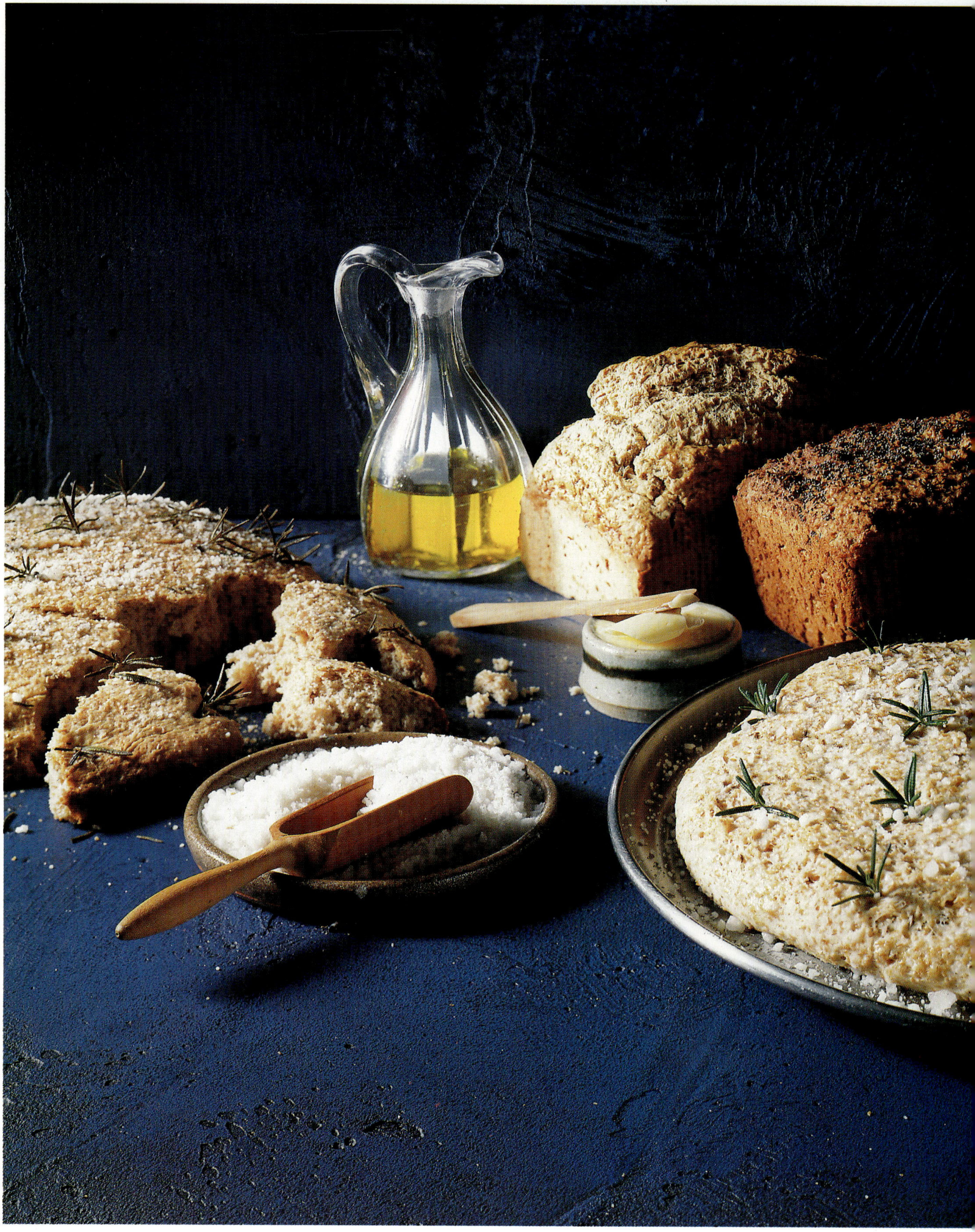

CHAPTER 9

BREAD

Bread really comes into its own at a braai. There are so many different ways of offering it that, whatever your time and energy restrictions may be, you can always put on a good show.

You may wish simply to heat a shop-bought French loaf, or mix up an instant number; perhaps impress your guests (and de-stress yourself) by kneading and baking a perfect yeast loaf, or rustle up a potbrood in the coals. Whatever your preference may be, here are some interesting recipes.

GARLIC BREAD

No-one will look askance if you present a shop-assembled garlic loaf, but here's how to do your own. If there's no time to peel and crush garlic, use dried flakes instead, but go easy as they're fairly pungent.

1 loaf French bread
100 g soft butter
3-4 cloves garlic, crushed

Preheat oven to 180 °C. Slice the bread fairly thickly. Mix together butter and garlic, spread liberally onto each slice, reform the loaf and wrap in heavy foil.

Bake for 15 minutes. Open foil along the top and return bread to the oven for a further 5-7 minutes to crisp.

To heat on the braai, warm the loaf gently on the grid over very low coals. Watch carefully as bread burns in a flash. Open the foil to crisp the crust towards the end of the warming time.
Makes 1 French loaf

Crusty Caraway and Rosemary Bread, Herbed Beer Bread, Farmhouse Loaf (pages 88–89)

VARIATION: GARLIC AND HERB BREAD
Scatter chopped fresh herbs liberally onto the garlic butter. My favourites are tarragon, marjoram or origanum and thyme mixed into chopped parsley. Dried herbs may be substituted, but don't use too much – they can be overpowering. A good idea is to mix a pinch of dried mixed herbs into freshly chopped parsley.

MAKE AHEAD
It's a great idea to always have Garlic Bread or Cheesy French Bread on hand for when unexpected guests drop in. Rustle up a couple of loaves, wrap them in foil and refrigerate for up to 3 days, or freeze for up to 3 months.

CHEESY FRENCH BREAD

A nice variation along the lines of garlic bread but with a tasty flavour twist.

1 loaf French bread
100 g soft butter
30 ml Dijon, French or coarse mustard
250 ml grated Gruyère or Cheddar cheese
4-6 spring onions, very finely sliced

Preheat oven to 150 °C. Slice loaf thickly, spread liberally with butter laced with mustard, then sprinkle with cheese and spring onions. Re-form the loaf, wrap in heavy foil and heat for 30-40 minutes. Open the top of the foil for the final 10 minutes to crisp the top.

When doing this loaf over the coals heat slowly, or the cheese will become tough and leathery. Open the foil to crisp the crust before serving.
Makes 1 French loaf

87

BRUSCHETTA

I love to offer these crisp breads with a choice of toppings – sliced tomato, fried brinjal, mozzarella cheese, salami, chopped olives – in fact anything that takes my fancy, though I draw the line at peanut butter and bacon.

1 small loaf Italian bread
olive oil
garlic cloves, peeled and halved

Preheat oven to 220 °C. Slice bread thinly, brush with olive oil, arrange on a baking tray and bake for 10-15 minutes until nice and crisp.

Rub each slice liberally with cut cloves of garlic and serve hot, or toast the bread on the grid over low coals. But watch it – bread burns in a trice and it's then no use to either man or beast.

HERBED BEER BREAD

A no-fuss loaf with a most unusual flavour that's quick to mix and bake.

750 ml cake or all-purpose flour
5 ml salt
15 ml baking powder
2 ml bicarbonate of soda
30 ml brown sugar
125 ml chopped dill or fennel
  or 15 ml dried dill or fennel
340 ml bottle beer

GLAZE
1 small egg
2 ml salt

Preheat oven to 160 °C. Grease a small loaf tin. Sift together flour, salt, baking powder and bicarb. Lightly mix in sugar and herbs. Pour in beer and knead lightly to form a stiff dough. (The whole procedure is quick-as-lick in a food processor, but please don't over-mix.)

Plop dough into the loaf tin, brush with combined egg and salt and bake for 60 minutes. Turn out and cool on a rack before serving with butter blended with fresh herbs.

Makes 1 small loaf

TOAST TOASTIES

Make these ahead or provide the wherewithal for everyone to assemble their own toasted sandwiches to cook over the coals. They are delicious as starters (to keep hunger pangs at bay) or served alongside suitable side-dishes with a more meaty slant.

Supply loads of sliced bread, butter, assorted fillings and hinged grids or jaffle irons in which to toast the treats.

FILLING SUGGESTIONS
(mushier ones more suited to jaffles)
☐ sliced cheese, tomato and onion
☐ grated cheese mixed with a drop of chutney
☐ stir-fried chopped onion, green pepper and tomato
☐ peanut butter and well-drained crumbled crispy bacon
☐ flaked cooked fish, tinned fish or slivered chicken with mayonnaise
☐ savoury mince
☐ mashed banana with ground cinnamon and sugar
☐ chopped dates, chopped nuts, lemon juice and a dash of yoghurt

VETKOEK

A beloved and infinitely fattening braai accompaniment. Serve with a sprinkling of salt with the main course, or add a tablespoonful of sugar to the mixture and offer as dessert, warm, with honey, syrup or jam.

500 ml cake or all-purpose flour
15 ml baking powder
2 ml salt
200 ml milk
1 egg, lightly beaten

Sift flour, baking powder and salt into a mixing bowl or into the bowl of a food processor. Mix together milk and egg and mix into the dry ingredients to make a well-blended dough.

Deep-fry in hot oil, using about 2 tablespoonfuls of dough for each vetkoek. When golden brown, drain well on kitchen paper and serve warm.

Makes about 12

SAVOURY BUTTERMILK BREAD

A quickly prepared loaf that is deliciously flavoured with a hint of heat.

100 g rindless streaky bacon
sunflower oil for cooking
375 ml wholewheat flour
250 ml cake or all-purpose flour
5 ml bicarbonate of soda
5 ml sugar
2 ml salt
5 ml dry English mustard
pinch of cayenne pepper
80 ml grated Parmesan cheese
1 egg, lightly beaten
500 ml buttermilk
15 ml Worcestershire sauce

Preheat oven to 160 °C. Grease a small loaf tin. Cook bacon until crisp in a little oil, drain, crumble and set aside. Tip wholewheat flour into a mixing bowl, sift in cake flour and bicarb, then add sugar, salt, mustard, cayenne pepper, cheese and bacon.

Combine egg, buttermilk and Worcestershire sauce and mix into dry ingredients. Spoon the mixture into the baking tin and bake for 60 minutes. Cool on a wire rack before serving.

Makes 1 small loaf

EASY WHITE BREAD

There's really no mystery about making white bread, and no need to be intimidated about the mixing/rising/punching down techniques described in the method. When you have turned out a perfect white loaf, you'll know what I mean.

750 ml cake or all-purpose flour
10 g sachet instant dried yeast
2 ml sugar
5 ml salt
15 ml sunflower oil
200 ml warm water (approximate amount)

Sift flour into a large mixing bowl. Mix in yeast, sugar and salt. Make a well in the centre and pour in oil and water. Mix to a nice dough (it may be necessary to add a little extra water), then knead for a few minutes until elastic.

Plop the dough into an oiled bowl, cover lightly with oiled clingfilm (this makes the dough draught-free and allows you to watch what's happening at the same time), and leave in a warm spot until doubled in bulk.

Punch down the dough, shape into a smooth oblong and place in a small, well greased loaf tin. Cover again lightly with oiled clingfilm and set aside in a warm spot to rise again until the dough peeps over the rim of the baking tin. Meanwhile preheat oven to 170 °C. Bake for 45 minutes until cooked (the loaf will sound hollow when tapped). Turn out to cool on a wire rack.
Makes 1 loaf

FARMHOUSE LOAF

A luxurious, traditional seed loaf. There's no need to follow the recipe slavishly; use whatever seeds you prefer, or omit them entirely when the budget is tight and increase the amount of wholewheat flour accordingly.

500 g (1 litre) wholewheat flour
150 g (250 ml) self-raising flour
250 ml molasses bran
60 ml sunflower seeds
60 ml sesame seeds
60 ml poppy seeds
60 ml linseeds
60 ml brown sugar
15 ml salt
30 ml sunflower oil
20 g (2 sachets) instant dried yeast
1 litre tepid water (approximate amount)
extra seed for decoration

Oil one large or two small loaf tins. Tip wholewheat flour into a large mixing bowl, sift in self-raising flour and add bran, seeds, sugar, salt, oil and yeast. Mix lightly but thoroughly, then add water and mix to a nice dough.

WATCHPOINT The amount of water required may vary, so don't add it all at once. When it is the correct consistency, the dough should plop off your hand back into the bowl.

Spoon dough into loaf tin/s and sprinkle extra seeds on the surface. Cover loosely with oiled clingfilm and leave in a warm, draught-free spot until the dough has doubled in bulk. Meanwhile preheat oven to 180 °C.

Remove clingfilm and bake bread for 40 minutes until it sounds hollow when tapped, then turn out on a rack to cool.
Makes 1 large or 2 small loaves

ROOSTERKOEK

Bread rolls cooked over low coals is a much-loved traditional side dish. Prepare any bread recipes but make sure the dough is on the stiff side (reduce the liquid). If not, it'll drip through onto the coals before the heat has time to crisp the outside.

Make sure the grid is sparkling clean. There's nothing more awful than your roosterkoek picking up bits of last week's braai as it cooks.

Shape bits of dough into small balls and place them on the grid. As soon as the undersides are crisp, turn and cook until they sound hollow when tapped. Cool slightly, then split and serve with butter.

CRUSTY CARAWAY AND ROSEMARY BREAD

If you're not mad about caraway seeds, use linseeds or poppy seeds instead.

1 litre white or brown bread flour
10 g sachet instant dried yeast
2 ml salt
15 ml caraway seeds
10 ml dried garlic flakes
15 ml sugar
100 ml water
250 ml milk
30 ml olive oil

TOPPING
olive oil
sea salt or coarse salt
fresh rosemary sprigs

Mix together flour, yeast, salt, caraway seeds, garlic and sugar.

Heat together water, milk and oil to blood temperature, add to dry ingredients and mix in well. Knead for a few minutes until the dough is nice and elastic. Place in a lightly oiled bowl, cover with oiled clingfilm and allow to rise in a warm, draught-free place until approximately doubled in bulk.

Knock down the dough, then form into a round, flattish shape. Place in a greased roasting tray, brush with olive oil, sprinkle with salt and spear with sprigs of rosemary. Cover and set aside again until doubled. Meanwhile preheat oven to 200 °C.

Bake bread for 15 minutes, then reduce oven temperature to 180 °C and bake for a further 25 minutes. Serve slightly warm and allow your guests to break off bits to eat with their fingers.
Makes 1 round loaf

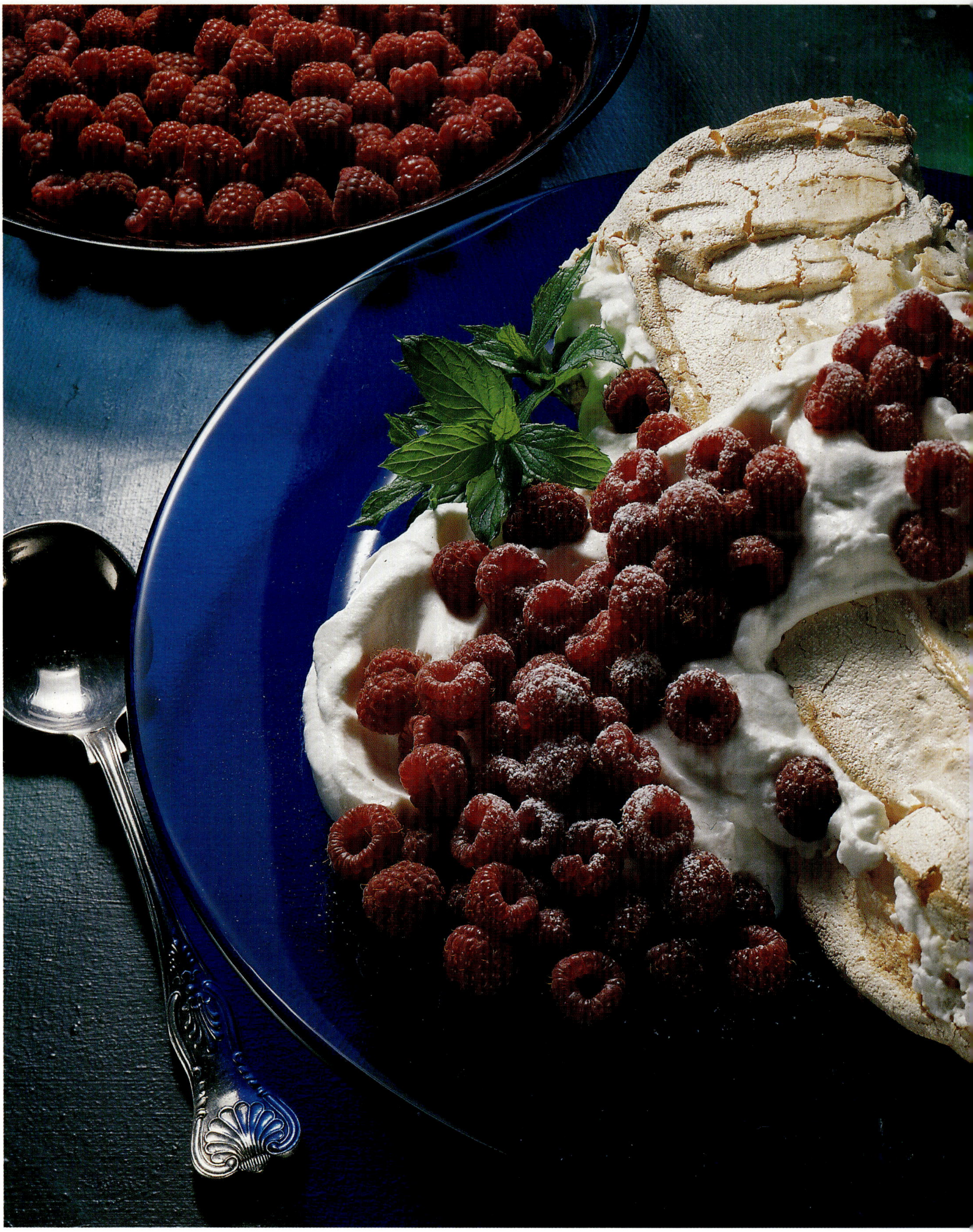

CHAPTER 10

DESSERT

A decadent dessert should be the ultimate indulgence for the host and all those enjoying the glow of the fire. So go ahead and prepare whatever turns you on; for sure, it'll enchant your guests too.

A prerequisite of a fireside pud is one that's quick and easy to make and needs little in the way of prissy presentation and last-minute pfaffing. Fruit, quickly whizzed up ice-creams, and tarts fit this bill beautifully, as do desserts which can be made ahead of time leaving you free to relax with your guests.

BANANA AND MARSHMALLOW PARCELS

This is kids' stuff that goes down well with grown-ups too. The assembled parcels may be stored in the fridge for up to a day.

4 ripe bananas
lemon juice
16 fat, squashy marshmallows
100 g dark or milk chocolate, grated

Butter 4 squares of heavy foil. Skin and slice bananas in half lengthwise. Place two halves in each piece of foil and top each with a squeeze of lemon juice, 4 marshmallows and a scattering of grated chocolate on top.

Close the foil and warm on the grid over the coolest coals for 10-15 minutes – just long enough to melt the marshmallows and chocolate. Don't cook over too fierce heat or longer than necessary as bananas toughen easily and the chocolate will harden. Serve from the parcels.
Serves 4

SKEWERED LYCHEES AND BANANAS WITH HOT CHOCOLATE SAUCE

Pretty as a picture, delicious to eat – and conveniently pre-preparable.

565 g tin pitted lychees
3 bananas
lemon juice

CHOCOLATE SAUCE
200 g dark chocolate
125 ml cream
30 ml coffee liqueur (optional)

TO SERVE
100 g toasted flaked almonds

Drain lychees. Peel and slice bananas into chunks and brush with lemon juice to prevent discolouring. Thread fruit onto skewers, cover and chill.

Gently heat together chocolate and cream in a bowl over simmering water and mix smoothly. Mix in liqueur.

Place kebabs on serving plates, pour ribbons of sauce over and garnish with toasted almonds.
Serves 6

MAKE AHEAD
The sauce is fine for several days. Reheat gently just before serving.

Rolled Pavlova with Fresh Berries (page 94)

FOILED FRUIT

Wrap fruit in foil and cook over the coals for a delicious and hassle-free dessert. What's more the parcels may be prepared a day ahead.

Foiled apples

Simply wash apples, wrap individually in buttered heavy foil and bake in the coolest section of the coals for at least 30 minutes or longer if you like. It's hard to spoil them.

An extra-special way is to core the apples and fill the cavities with a mixture of chopped nuts, brown sugar, cinnamon, soft butter and a squeeze of lemon juice. Or fill with fruit mince softened with a splosh of brandy before wrapping in foil.

These mushy treats are best eaten with a spoon directly from the foil. But let them cool down first – straight from the fire they're hot as hell!

Foiled mixed fruit

Peel and thickly slice banana, cut fresh pineapple into chunks, and skin and slice melon or paw paw. Divide the fruit between sheets of heavy foil with a light sprinkling of brown sugar and a dash of brandy or Van der Hum.

Place parcels on the grid over the coolest part of the coals while the main course is being served. They'll be ready when you are.

ICED BERRY WHIP

Any seasonal berries may be used. Or make several different types of whips and serve varying scoops together on one platter, garnished with sprigs of mint and extra fresh berries.

500 g ripe berries, washed and hulled
250 g (300 ml) castor sugar
500 ml cream

Blend together berries and sugar. Whip cream until soft peaks form, fold in and freeze in a suitable container.
Makes 2 litres

GLAZED FRUIT KEBABS

These interesting diversions may be served hot or cool, either with the meat if it warrants a fruity garnish, or for dessert with a dollop of whipped cream.

SUITABLE FRUIT
peach segments
guava chips
halved apricots
cherries
pear slices
apple wedges
halved nectarines
banana slices
plum pieces

MARINADE AND GLAZE
125 ml orange juice
125 ml semi-sweet white wine
45 ml honey
45 ml fruit-based liqueur (Curaçao, Van der Hum, Grand Marnier or Cointreau)

Allow 36-48 chunks of fruit and thread them onto six thin bamboo skewers. Place side-by-side in a non-metallic dish.

Combine marinade ingredients and heat gently just until the honey melts. Pour over kebabs, turning them to coat evenly. Marinate for several hours until dessert time, then braai over hot coals for 2-3 minutes on each side, brushing with the remaining marinade to glaze.
Serves 6

HALVA ICE-CREAM

Not a soul in the world will know that this delicious dessert is whizzed up so easily.

2 litres vanilla ice-cream
200 g halva

Allow ice-cream to soften a little then blend in a food processor with half the halva. Crumble remaining halva, fold in gently and re-freeze. Serve scoops with small, crunchy biscuits.
Makes about 1,5 litres; 8 servings

QUICK LEMON ICE-CREAM

This light and tangy braai-ender is one of the easiest ice-creams to make.

250 ml milk
250 ml cream
200 ml castor sugar
finely grated rind of 1 lemon
juice of two lemons

Whip milk, cream and castor sugar in a food processor until smooth. Pour into a freezer-friendly container and place in the freezer until it's half frozen.

Re-whip with the lemon rind and juice, then re-freeze as before. Whip once more when the mixture is half frozen then freeze solid.
Serves 4-6

CHOCOLATE VELVET ICE-CREAM

Chocoholics will adore this dessert, especially as it's easy to make.

250 ml castor sugar
200 ml cocoa powder
100 g slab dark chocolate, broken into blocks
125 ml strong black coffee
500 ml cream
3 egg yolks

TOPPING
grated dark chocolate

In a small saucepan combine castor sugar, cocoa, chocolate, coffee, and 125 ml of the cream. Stir over low heat until smoothly blended and the mixture comes to the boil. In a food processor or mixer whip egg yolks until pale and thickened, then whiz in the hot chocolate. Allow the mixture to cool to room temperature before continuing.

Whip 250 ml of the cream until thick enough to hold soft peaks, then fold this into the chocolate mixture. Spoon into individual serving bowls or glasses and freeze – for up to a month if necessary.

TO SERVE Just before serving whip remaining cream until slightly thickened (don't make it too thick) and pour a little onto each serving. Garnish with a generous scattering of grated chocolate.
Serves 8

CARAMEL PEPPERMINT CRUNCH PUDDING

A great dessert for a crowd – an appealing layered pud with a minty crunch. It may be made ahead in the serving bowl, whipped out of the fridge and quickly tizzied up just before serving.

400 g tin condensed milk
400 g tin evaporated milk, well chilled
10 ml gelatine
200 g packet crunchy biscuits
2 large Peppermint Crisps

GARNISH
whipped cream

Boil the unopened tin of condensed milk in water for an hour to caramelise. Chill.

Measure 60 ml of the evaporated milk in a cup, sprinkle gelatine on top and stand it in hot water until gelatine dissolves. Or microwave for 30 seconds on full power. Stir and allow to cool.

Whip remaining evaporated milk until thick and foamy. Add the caramel little by little. Blend in gelatine and refrigerate pudding for about 30 minutes until it starts to set. Meanwhile crush biscuits and Peppermint Crisps together.

Stir the pudding, then layer it with the biscuit/chocolate mixture in a large glass bowl. Refrigerate for an hour or two to set. Just before serving garnish with piped cream.
Serves 10-12

MAKE AHEAD
Unfortunately, the biscuity chocolate layer tends to get a bit soft and soggy after languishing for more than a day in the fridge, so prepare the pud no more than 24 hours ahead.

MOCHA MALLOW MOUSSE

Otherwise known as 'cheat's chocolate mousse', this is a recipe for those who like something light and luscious, and who don't have overmuch time to spare in the kitchen whipping up a traditional and time-consuming mousse. This is far cheaper too.

400 g tin evaporated milk, well chilled
200 g dark chocolate, broken into blocks
200 g white marshmallows *

GARNISH
250 ml cream
1 small Flake chocolate

* *Make sure they're the big, squashy ones; these contain more gelatine to lighten and set the pud.*

Measure 125 ml of the evaporated milk into the top of a double boiler and add chocolate and marshmallows. Melt together over simmering water, mixing until well blended. Allow to cool or you'll run the risk of the dessert deflating.

Whisk remaining evaporated milk until thick enough to hold soft peaks (it won't whip well if it isn't cold enough), fold in chocolaty marshmallow mixture thoroughly, pour the mixture into a glass bowl and chill for 3-4 hours to set.

Decorate with whipped cream and crumbled chocolate before serving.
Serves 8-10

MAKE AHEAD
Prepare the dessert a day or two ahead, but don't decorate until about 4 hours before serving. The cream will harden in the fridge.

FLAMING BANANAS

Sizzle up over the coals and serve with a scoop of ice-cream.

4-6 bananas
lemon juice
50 g (50 ml) butter
45 ml brown sugar
60 ml brandy
juice of 1 orange

Peel bananas, slice lengthwise and squeeze lemon juice over. Fry in sizzling butter until lightly browned – using a non-stick frying-pan is best.

Sprinkle with sugar, pour over brandy and flame. Add orange juice and cook quickly until sauce is syrupy – but take care not to let the bananas get mushy.
Serves 4

QUICK CHEESECAKE

The simplest cheesecake prepared in a flash – and polished off just as fast.

NUTTY BISCUIT CRUST
100 g brazil nuts, very finely chopped
200 g crisp biscuits, crushed
200 ml desiccated coconut
60 ml sugar
125 g butter, melted

FILLING
400 g tin condensed milk
2 x 250 g tubs cream cheese (or smooth cottage cheese)
125 ml lemon juice

GARNISH
250 ml cream
grated lemon rind

Preheat oven to 180 °C. Lightly oil a 24 cm springform baking tin, deep flan tin or quiche tin. Mix together crust ingredients and press into the base and sides. Bake for 10 minutes. Allow to cool.

Combine filling ingredients, pour into crust and chill until set. Garnish with piped cream and grated lemon rind.
Serves 10-12

DESSERT

LEMON MERINGUE PIE

Here's a trip down memory lane — an all-time family favourite. Lovely stuff for those with a real sweet tooth who enjoy an occasional nostaliga trip.

BISCUIT CRUST
400 g crisp biscuits
125 g butter, melted

FILLING
2 x 400 g tins full-cream condensed milk *
4 XL or jumbo eggs, separated
30 ml lemon juice **
30 ml castor sugar

* Don't use low-fat condensed milk; the filling won't set.
** Use only juice from ripe yellow lemons; the juice of green lemons will cause the filling to separate.

Preheat oven to 180 °C. Butter a 25 cm pie plate or quiche tin. Crush biscuits, mix with melted butter and press into the prepared baking dish. Bake for 15-20 minutes until lightly browned and crisp. Allow to cool before adding the filling.

Mix together condensed milk, egg yolks and lemon juice. Pour into the pastry shell and chill well.

Whisk egg whites until stiff enough to form peaks. Beat in castor sugar little by little to form a stiff, glossy mixture. Pile onto the pie and brown under a preheated oven griller. Watch all the while – it burns in a flash.
Serves 10-12

VARIATION
Substitute the biscuit crust with the slightly more elaborate crust given for Quick Cheesecake (page 93).

MAKE AHEAD
Complete the pie a day or two before serving, but don't add the meringue topping until the very last minute. If made too far ahead, the meringue gets wrinkled and collapses in a heap (a sorry state of affairs for all concerned!). Serve straight from the oven.

CHOCOLATE CRISPY TART

A chocolate mousse-type filling in the crispiest crust imaginable. It's great for a crowd and best on the day it's made. Serve with softly whipped cream.

CRUST
100 g dark chocolate
50 g (50 ml) butter
50 g Rice Krispies

FILLING
250 ml milk
60 ml castor sugar
2 eggs, separated
15 ml gelatine
300 g dark chocolate, broken into blocks
30 ml brandy (optional)
250 ml cream

CRUST   Melt chocolate and butter over simmering water. Remove from the heat, mix in Rice Krispies and press the mixture into the base and sides of a 23 cm deep pie dish or quiche tin. Chill to set nice and firm.
FILLING   In a medium saucepan (or a double boiler, if you're nervous about the custard curdling) combine milk, sugar and egg yolks. Stir over medium heat until the custard thickens sufficiently to coat the back of the spoon. Remove from the heat, sprinkle gelatine onto the surface and mix in well. Add chocolate and stir until melted. Stir in brandy. Cool the custard to room temperature.

Whisk egg whites until they hold soft peaks. Whisk cream separately then fold both into chocolate base carefully and thoroughly. Pour into pie crust and refrigerate until set – at least 2 hours.
Serves 12

ROLLED PAVLOVA WITH FRESH BERRIES

A pretty pud that goes a long way. If berries are unavailable use sliced bananas or well drained mandarin oranges. It's essential to weigh the castor sugar accurately to get the correct texture, ever so slightly crisp on the outside and soft within.

6 egg whites
375 g castor sugar
20 ml cornflour
5 ml vanilla essence

FILLING
250 ml tub cream
300 g fresh berries

GARNISH
extra whipped cream
mint sprigs

Preheat oven to 200 °C. Line a 30 cm x 45 cm baking tin with foil and spray lightly with oil. On your working surface lay a damp tea towel and cover it with a sheet of waxed paper.

Whisk egg whites with an electric mixer until very stiff. Mix together castor sugar and cornflour and add this a little at a time, beating well after each addition. Add vanilla and whisk for a minute or two more until the mixture is glossy. Spread it fairly evenly onto prepared baking tin, leaving space around the edge to allow the meringue to spread while cooking. Bake for 12 minutes, remove from the oven and turn pavlova onto the waxed paper. Peel off the foil and allow to cool.

Whip cream stiffly, spread it onto the meringue and top with fruit. Roll up in the tea towel starting from the long side. Place on a suitable serving dish, garnish with whipped cream and sprigs of mint.
Serves 10-12

MAKE AHEAD
This is best served immediately after filling and rolling, but refrigerating the completed dish for a couple of hours doesn't do it too much harm. The meringue may be baked up to 8 hours before filling but don't refrigerate, it'll get sticky.

INDEX

A
Alikreukels 53
Anchovy:
    and olive butter 26
    dressing with nut and feta slaw 73
    with Italian peppers 16
Antipasto, Italian 16
Apples:
    and celery and pecan salad 73
    foiled 92
Apricot glaze 32
Artichokes with balsamic
    vinaigrette 15
Asado 58
Asparagus, fresh with citrus
    mayonnaise 15

B
Baby chickens, tuckered 42
Bacon bananas 74
Baconed kidney kebabs 45
Bananas:
    and marshmallow parcels 91
    and skewered lychees with
      hot chocolate sauce 91
    bacon bananas 74
    banana beans 77
    braaied 74
    flaming 93
Barbecue sauce 69
Basting sauces: see Marinades
Beans:
    and lentils with herb vinaigrette 78
    banana beans 77
    big bean mix 78
    sousboontjies 78
    Yankee baked 78
Beef potjie 64
Beef 25
    garlic T-bone 25
    homespun hamburgers 26
    Indonesian satay 26
    marinated beef fillet 25
    rump steak with olive and
      anchovy butter 26
    steaks with blue cheese stuffing 26
Berry whip, iced 92
Blackened fish with spiced cucumber
    yoghurt 52
Boerewors 47
Bread 87
    bruschetta 88
    cheesy French 87
    crusty caraway and rosemary 89
    easy white 89
    farmhouse 89
    garlic 87
    herbed beer 88
    roosterkoek 89
    savoury buttermilk 88
    toast toasties 88
    vetkoek 88

Brinjal and onion pickle 79
Brinjals Niçoise 80
Bruschetta 88
Butter:
    clarified 16
    garlic 22
    olive and anchovy 26
Butterflied lamb 31
Butternut, foil-baked 76

C
Cabbage:
    and celery, marinated 72
    coleslaw 73
    nut and feta slaw 73
Caesar salad 72
Caramel peppermint crunch
    pudding 93
Cauliflower and tomatoes,
    crumbed 80
Cheesy chicken in bacon 41
Cheesy French bread 87
Cheesy onions 81
Cheesecake 93
Chicken 41
    charred fillets with tomato and
      coriander salsa 41
    cheesy chicken with bacon 41
    oriental chicken skewers 41
    honey-glazed breasts 42
    flaming chicken 42
    potjie, boozy 62
    potjie, Mediterranean 62
    tuckered baby chickens 42
Chicken liver kebabs 45
Chicken liver pâté, herbed 16
Chinese spareribs 36
Chocolate crispy tart 94
Chocolate velvet ice-cream 92
Chops:
    minty 31
    tarragon 39
Clarified butter 16
Coleslaw 73
    nut and feta 73
Crayfish 54
Cucumber:
    spiced yoghurt 52
    Szechwan 15
Cutlets with peppered mushroom
    sauce 39

D
Dessert 91
    banana and marshmallow
      parcels 91
    caramel peppermint crunch 93
    chocolate crispy tart 94
    chocolate velvet ice-cream 92
    flaming bananas 93
    foiled fruit 92

    glazed fruit kebabs 92
    halva ice-cream 92
    iced berry whip 92
    lemon meringue pie 94
    mocha mallow mousse 93
    quick cheesecake 93
    quick lemon ice-cream 92
    rolled pavlova with fresh
      berries 94
    skewered lychees and bananas
      with hot chocolate sauce 91
Dijon pork steaks 35

F
Figs in bacon 74
Fish: see also Seafood 49
    blackened with spiced cucumber
      yoghurt 52
    fillets, braaied 50
    fillets with mushrooms and
      almonds 52
    in foil 50
    plough disc fish 50
    skewered tiddlers 52
    whole fish on the braai 50

G
Gammon with pineapple, glazed 35
Garlic:
    bread 87
    butter 22
    coal-roasted 78
    prawns 54
    T-bone 25
Gem squash, foil-baked 76
Glazed gammon with pineapple 35
Glazed onions with tomato and
    coriander 81
Greek salad 72
Green peppercorn sauce 69
Green salad 72
Guinea fowl, old-fashioned
    potjie 63

H
Hamburgers, homespun 26
Herb mayonnaise 68
Honey:
    and herb mix 22
    and soy vinaigrette 67
    honeyed curry baste 39
    -glazed chicken breasts 42
Horseradish sauce 68

I
Ice-cream:
    chocolate velvet 92
    halva 92
    quick lemon 92

K
Kachoomer 71
Kebabs:
    baconed kidney 45
    chicken liver with bacon,
      pineapple and peppers 45
    pork with orange and brandy
      baste 36
Kidney, baconed kebabs 45
Krummelpap 62

L
Lamb 31
    minty chops 31
    loin of lamb with garlic
      and rosemary 31
    butterflied lamb 31
    boning a leg of 32
    rolled lamb with pineapple
      stuffing 32
    Siamese satay 32
    shish kebabs 32
    sosaties 33
    soutribbetjies 33
    spit-roast 57
Langoustines 54
Lemon:
    ice-cream 92
    meringue pie 94
Lentils and beans with herb
    vinaigrette 78
Liver:
    chicken liver kebabs with bacon,
      pineapple and peppers 45
    herbed chicken liver pâté 16
    over the coals with onion 45
Lobster 54
Lychees and bananas, with hot
    chocolate sauce 91

M
Marinades and basting sauces:
    garlic butter 22
    herbs and honey 22
    Mandarin 23
    Mediterranean herb and
      orange 22
    peachy 22
    sizzling 23
    tarragon 39
Marinated beef fillet 25
Marinated mushrooms 77
Marinated olives and feta 13
Mayonnaise 68
    citrus 15
    herb 68
    pesto 68
    tapenade 68
Mealies, braaied 76
Meat 19
Mediterranean chicken potjie 62

Mushrooms:
　braaied 77
　filled with spicy rice 77
　mozzarella mushrooms with herbed tomato 77
Mussels 53
　parcels 53

N
Noodle, oriental salad 73
Nuts, roasted mixed 13

O
Offal 45
　baconed kidney kebabs 45
　chicken liver kebabs with bacon, pineapple and peppers 45
　liver over the coals with onion 45
Old man sauce 69
Olives and feta, marinated 13
Onions:
　herbed orange and olive salad 71
　and brinjal pickle 79
　cheesy 81
　foil-baked 76
　glazed with tomato and coriander 81
　slaphakskeentjies 81
　sweet and sour 85
Orange:
　and brandy baste 36
　and herb baste 22
　herbed orange, onion and olive salad 71
Oxtail potjie 63

P
Parlsey-pasted venison 29
Pâté, herbed chicken liver 16
Pavlova, rolled with fresh berries 94
Peppers, Italian 16
Perlemoen 52
　in kelp 53
　parcels 53
Pesto mayonnaise 68
Pork 35
　Chinese spareribs 36
　Dijon pork steaks 35
　fillet with bacon and banana 36
　glazed gammon with pineapple 35
　kebabs with orange and brandy baste 36
　sausages, herbed 47
　spiced pork loin 36
　with minted apple 35
Pork sausages, herbed 47
Potatoes:
　and cottage cheese bake 84
　and onion parcel 84
　baked 82
　garlicky potato and onion with rosemary 85
　herbed potato fry 85
　hot potato salad 85
　orange-glazed sweet potato 84
　salad 84

Potbrood 62
Potjiekos 61
　beef 64
　boozy chicken 62
　Mediterranean chicken 62
　old-fashioned guinea fowl 63
　oxtail 63
　pumpkin 61
　seafood 64
　turkey with spicy rice stuffing 64
Prawns 54
　spiked garlic 54
Pumpkin in a potjie 61

R
Ratatouille 81
Rice, dirty 82
Rice salad 82
Roasted braai spice 22
Roasted mixed nuts 13
Roosterkoek 89

S
Satay:
　Indonesian 26
　sauce 69
　Siamese 32
Sauces and dressings 67
　barbecue sauce 69
　tomato and coriander salsa 68
　green peppercorn sauce 69
　herb vinaigrette 67
　herbed tomato sauce 68
　honey and soy vinaigrette 67
　mayonnaise 68
　　citrus 15
　　herb 68
　　pesto 68
　　tapenade 68
　horseradish sauce 68
　old man sauce 69
　quick satay sauce 69
　seafood sauce 68
　spicy yoghurt dressing 68
　tartare sauce 68
　vinaigrette 67
Sausage 47
　boerewors 47
　herbed pork 47
Schnitzels with ham and cheese 39
Seafood 49
　alikreukels 53
　blackened fish with spiced cucumber yoghurt 52
　crayfish 54
　fish 49
　fish fillets with mushrooms and almonds 52
　mixed seafood parcels 54
　mussels 53
　mussel parcels 53
　perlemoen 52
　perlemoen in kelp 53
　perlemoen parcels 53
　prawns and langoustines 54
　seafood potjie 64
　skewered tiddlers 52
　spiked garlic prawns 54

Seven spice mix 22
Shish kebabs 32
Siamese satay 32
Side dishes 71
　apple, celery and pecan salad 73
　bacon bananas 74
　baked potatoes 82
　banana beans 77
　big bean mix 78
　braaied bananas 74
　braaied mealies 76
　braaied mushrooms 77
　marinated mushrooms 77
　brinjal and onion pickle 79
　Caesar salad 72
　charred vegetables 74
　cheesy onions 81
　coal-roasted garlic 78
　coleslaw 73
　crumbed cauliflower and tomatoes 80
　dirty rice 82
　figs in bacon 74
　foil-baked vegetables 76
　　onions 76
　　butternut 76
　　gem squash 76
　garlicky potato and onion with rosemary 85
　glazed onions with tomatoes and coriander 81
　great green salad 72
　great potato salad 84
　Greek salad 72
　herbed orange, onion and olive salad 71
　herbed potato fry 85
　hot potato salad 85
　hot spinach salad with bacon and mushrooms 74
　kachoomer 71
　lentils and beans with herb vinaigrette 78
　marinated cabbage and celery 72
　mozzarella mushrooms with herbed tomato 77
　mushrooms filled with spicy rice 77
　Niçoise brinjals 80
　nut and feta slaw with anchovy dressing 73
　orange-glazed sweet potato 84
　oriental noodle and nut salad 73
　potato and cottage cheese bake 84
　potato and onion parcel 84
　ratatouille 81
　rice salad 82
　slaphakskeentjies 81
　sousboontjies 78
　stir-fried spinach with bacon, tomatoes and feta 74
　sweet and sour onions 85
　sweetcorn fritters 76
　vegetable kebabs 76
　Yankee baked beans 78
Skewered tiddlers 52
Slaphakskeentjies 81
Sosaties 33
Soutribbetjies 33

Spareribs, Chinese 36
Spicy yoghurt dressing 68
Spinach:
　hot salad with bacon and mushrooms 74
　stir-fried with bacon, tomatoes and feta 74
Spitroast 57
　lamb 57
　pig 58
Starters 13
　artichokes with balsamic vinaigrette 15
　fresh asparagus with citrus mayonnaise 15
　herbed chicken liver pâté 16
　hot tomato toasts 17
　Italian antipasto 16
　Italian peppers with anchovies 16
　marinated olives and feta 13
　roasted mixed nuts 13
　Szechwan cucumbers 15
　tomato and mozzarella with basil vinaigrette 16
Steak:
　with blue cheese stuffing 26
　with olive and anchovy butter 26
Stir-fried spinach with bacon, tomatoes and feta 74
Stywepap 61
Sweetcorn fritters 76
Sweet potato, orange-glazed 84
Szechwan cucumbers 15

T
Tapenade mayonnaise 68
Tarragon chops 39
Tartare sauce 68
Toast toasties 88
Tomato:
　and coriander salsa 41
　and crumbed cauliflower 80
　and mozzarella with basil vinaigrette 16
　herbed sauce 68
　toasts, hot 17
Turkey in a potjie with spicy rice stuffing 64

V
Veal 39
　cutlets with peppered mushroom sauce 39
　tarragon chops 39
　schnitzels with ham and cheese 39
Venison 29
　parsley-pasted 29
　boned leg of 29
Vegetables:
　charred 74
　foil-baked 76
　kebabs 76
Vetkoek 88
Vinaigrette 67
　balsamic 15
　basil 16
　herb 67
　honey and soy 67

96　INDEX